Every Day Is A

Character Day

Activity Book

FERNE PRESS

Kris Yankee and Marian Nelson

Every Day Is A Character Day Activity Book for the **Becoming a Better You!** series

Copyright © 2015 by Kris Yankee and Marian Nelson

Layout and cover design by Jacqueline L. Challiss Hill
Illustrations by Jeff Covieo
Illustrations created with digital graphics
"H5 Look at My Face" illustrations created by Jacqueline L. Challiss Hill

Printed in the United States of America

Summary: An activity book that complements the **Becoming a Better You!** book series.
Library of Congress Cataloging-in-Publication Data
Yankee, Kris and Nelson, Marian
Every Day Is A Character Day Activity Book/Kris Yankee and Marian Nelson–First Edition
ISBN-13: 978-1-938326-48-6
1. Honesty. 2. Self-respect. 3. Character education. 4. Self-esteem. 4. Elementary education.
I. Yankee, Kris and Nelson, Marian II. Title
Library of Congress Control Number: 2015910815

Resting heartbeat vs. working heartrate
http://www.heart.org/HEARTORG/GettingHealthy/PhysicalActivity/FitnessBasics/
Target-Heart-Rates_UCM_434341_Article.jsp

Word definitions from www.macmillandictionary.com

Word Searches created using wordsearchlabs.com © Matt Johnson

FERNE PRESS

Ferne Press is an imprint of Nelson Publishing & Marketing
366 Welch Road, Northville, MI 48167
www.nelsonpublishingandmarketing.com
(248) 735-0418

Table of Contents

Dear Educator 6
Introduction 7
How to Begin/A Healthy and Caring Classroom Climate 8

Confident 9
MONDAY is all about being CONFIDENT!
- Bring on the confidence! 10
- I am organized! 11
- Do your best! 12
- We all make mistakes 13
- Let's work together 14
- Let's solve problems 15
- Let's try something new 16
- How do you talk to yourself? 17
- Being prepared 18
- Donate your time 19
- Working hard in your community (service learning) 20
- Being a true friend 21
- What it takes to be a good leader 22
- Nobody's perfect 23
- How can you show others support? 24

Respect 25
TUESDAY is all about being RESPECTFUL!
- Bring on the respect! 26
- How can we show respect to our parents and others? 27
- Open your ears and listen! 28
- Being careful with others' belongings 29
- Paying attention shows a lot to others 30
- Hey...shhh! 31
- Taking your turn 32
- Following directions 33
- How do you treat yourself? 34
- How do you solve problems? 35
- Spending time with grandparents and other family members 36
- Family events 37
- Taking responsibility for your behavior 38
- Taking care of the environment 39
- How we treat each other 40

Empathy

Empathy 41

WEDNESDAY is all about being EMPATHETIC!

- Bring on the empathy! 42
- Helping family members and others 43
- Listening to a friend 44
- Helping another person.. 45
- Asking for help to improve your grades 46
- Being in a new situation 47
- How can you help a hurt or injured friend? 48
- How to make a difference in someone's life 49
- Think before you speak and act 50
- Listening closely because you may learn something new 51
- Giving makes a difference 52
- Listening to a friend shows you care 53
- Participating in a service-learning project 54
- Being a good sport 55
- Be aware of how others are feeling and show kindness 56

Honest

Honest 57

THURSDAY is all about being HONEST!

- Bring on the honesty! 58
- Answering parents truthfully... 59
- Asking for help 60
- Thinking about the feelings of a friend 61
- Think before you make a mistake like cheating 62
- What happens when you lie? 63
- Paying for things 64
- Being honest when working on a service-learning project 65
- Making the right choice... 66
- Being a reliable person 67
- Taking something that you want.. 68
- Returning something that doesn't belong to you and admitting your mistake 69
- Following the rules 70
- Playing fair 71
- How would you feel if you stole something but didn't get caught? 72

Grateful

Grateful 73

FRIDAY is all about being GRATEFUL!

- Bring on the gratefulness! 74
- What are you grateful for? 75
- How can you show gratefulness to your family and others? 76
- Showing gratefulness to animals 77
- How will school help you succeed? 78
- Discover your talents! 79
- What words do you use to show gratefulness toward yourself? 80
- What words and actions do you use to show gratefulness toward others? 81
- What do you do when you want something? 82
- We are grateful when friends support us 83
- Being a good role model 84
- Having pride of ownership 85
- Teamwork! 86
- Working on partner projects 87
- How can you help a sibling or friend? 88

H5 Skills Pages 89

Common Core Standards and Social Emotional Learning Strategies Aligned 139

About the Authors 143

Dear Educator,

Thank you for recognizing the importance of character education!

Why is character so critical?

We are convinced that positive character builds the foundation for a successful life. In the High 5 for Character world, our formula for success is head + hands + heart = happiness. We know that a good balance of academic learning and character learning will develop a well-rounded child.

As parents, we want our own children to grow up to be happy, successful, and purposeful people. We believe that educators want the same for their students. Teachers have the profound job of integrating character in the classroom. Building positive character will have an impact on their students' lives.

Our **Becoming a Better You!** series lays the groundwork for achievement through books centered around the themes of confidence, respect, empathy, honesty, and gratefulness.

Why do we believe it starts with confidence?

At High 5 for Character, it is vital that kids build confidence in themselves as a strong foundation to the other four character traits. If we don't believe in ourselves, can we be respectful toward or believe in someone else? No. Confident people are more inclined to be respectful, empathetic, honest, and grateful toward others and themselves. You will notice that throughout the book series we have also included themes like responsibility, trust, citizenship, caring, and fairness.

This activity book is filled with hundreds of ways to incorporate five- to ten-minute lessons into your daily curriculum. By repeated focus on positive character, you will be ingraining these messages into the students' outlook on life. For instance, if the book you're referring to is *Are You Confident Today?*, take every opportunity to focus on and reinforce students' confident behavior.

You have the tools. It's up to you. Kids are worth it. Now, go for it!

High-fives,
Kris Yankee and *Marian Nelson*

For more information or to order books and related products, please visit www.high5forcharacter.com. Contact us at 248.735.0418 and high5forcharacter@gmail.com.

Introduction

We see many aspects of good and bad character each day in children and adults. This program is designed to focus on the traits of our **Becoming a Better You!** five-book series, but you will notice that integrated into each book are other concepts such as trust, responsibility, citizenship, fairness, and caring. Our program works well with other previously instituted programs such as The Leader in Me™, Character Counts!™, Character.org™, and CharacterPlus™.

Establish a brief time at the beginning of each day to focus on the daily theme. We call it a "Character Chat." It sets the stage for the day. Then throughout the day, look for ways to reinforce the concept as a skill for each child. These may be reminders, situations that occur during the day, recess behavior, or after school activities.

The most profound words you can say are, "You can do this. I am here for you. I believe you can." When kids know that they have someone rooting for them, they will try harder. If you say, "Report back to me. I want to know how it turns out," you are showing them that you care. More than ever, kids need to know that someone cares.

Somewhere along the way, a disconnect has occurred where kids are feeling more stress, are feeling less connected, and have a lack of hope. Less talking is happening in families. Vital character skills are not being taught and reinforced. Kids need us. They need to know that they matter. That is where teachers come in.

Can we measure great character? Many school districts across the country are measuring test scores, detention, expulsions, referrals, behavior problems, and more. The school districts that have a strong character framework are finding that there is a huge decrease in referrals, lunch/recess problems, detention, bus problems, and more.

Build your team! Each classroom has the opportunity to be the best. Love your kids and teach them how to love you. When this happens, they will succeed.

How to Begin

Using our activity book is easy!

We feel the best use of this book is to highlight one of the five character traits each day of the week. We've set the book up with confidence on Monday, respect on Tuesday, empathy on Wednesday, honesty on Thursday, and gratefulness on Friday. Each day of the week can be used to emphasize each character trait.

If you are looking for a more in-depth study, you can use the fifteen themes in each of the five books for a three-week intense character trait study. There are actually ninety lessons for each character trait with a total of four hundred fifty lessons for all five character traits. A class could easily spend five to six weeks on a character trait before moving on to the next one.

There are many lessons to choose from on each activity page. Pick one or two and find out what works for you. We encourage you to work through the activity book in the order in which it is presented. Always remember to read the book first to the students. You'll notice that each section has a "Bring on …" page that introduces the book, the character trait, and the corresponding mantra. This is an excellent place to start. Saying the mantra every morning will help solidify and keep the students' focus on the overall theme. For the first five activities of each theme, we give you the language to use when presenting each lesson. **Practice on Your Own** is designed to build personal experiences that reinforce the concept either in or out of the classroom. The **H5 High 5ver**! form is designed to be used as a reinforcement of positive character. This form can be filled out by anyone (e.g., teacher, student, paraprofessional, etc.) and then turned in to the teacher who can read it at the end of the day or the following morning during Character Chat.

Each student should have a dedicated character folder so that all of the H5 Skill Pages can be stored and then referred to as needed. We want the kids to be able to go back and revisit the pages after the series is completed the first time so kids can see if growth has taken place.

A Healthy and Caring Classroom Climate

- Look for opportunities to encourage confidence in kids.
- Use the word "confident" in conversations with kids, e.g., "I am confident that you all make great choices."
- Character is about massaging the heart. When we say and do nurturing things, we are nurturing our hearts and strengthening the heart muscle.
- Build your classroom climate around character. Look for the positive aspects throughout the day where kids build each other up and show support. Point them out.
- You are the classroom leader. Your attitude and behavior will set the pace for developing a loving, caring climate.

Confident

How can I teach confidence today?

Thank you for seeing the vital importance of building character in the children in your classroom. We are excited to share our materials with you, in the hope that you will incorporate character education in each child every day.

We believe that when kids are confident about who they are and what they can do, they will feel sure of themselves. Academic learning is about learning new things. When kids feel confident, they are more apt to try new things and keep working on them until they master the concepts. Confidence requires a lot of reinforcement by adults and peers. This reinforcement will reduce the fear, reluctance to try, and chances of giving up. When children see that they have the power to believe in themselves, each experience they have will be a learning opportunity to reinforce how they feel the next time.

Words and phrases that you can use in your classroom:
- "Learn from your mistake and try again."
- "Instead of saying, 'I can't,' try saying, 'I will try' instead."
- "Nobody's perfect."
- "Do your best on everything you attempt."
- "Practice and never give up!"

Encourage healthy body language:
- Smile
- Make eye contact
- Stand up straight

MONDAY is all about being CONFIDENT!

Theme: Bring on the confidence!

Read this book before you begin.

Find the definition of the character trait (confidence).

Have the kids name five ways to be confident as shown in the book. Post answers for all to see.

Try This!
Have all kids repeat the mantra on this page five times out loud: **"I'm ready to do my best!"**

Character question: How do they feel after repeating the mantra? This mantra is to help kids feel empowered to do their best. Teachers can encourage kids that each should be doing their best all day.

End of Day Character Challenge: What was the mantra they said in the morning? "I'm ready to do my best." Give high-fives to all students.

Try this!
Each day when you wake up,
say out loud,
"I'm ready to do my best."

Theme: I am organized!

You are organized! You pack your own backpack for school. Your mom doesn't have to ask if you're prepared for the day. She is confident you're ready.

Discussion: What does being organized have to do with being confident? (When we are organized, we are prepared for the day: e.g., pack your backpack the night before so you don't have to worry about it the next morning.) Being organized starts at home and goes throughout the day. Have kids give two examples of how their confidence soars all day.

Compare & Contrast: Discuss what happens when we are and aren't prepared for the day. Use the **H5 T-Chart Skills Page** (pg. 131) to chart being organized and being disorganized (i.e., being ready for a test, soccer game, etc.).

— ⋅⋅⋅⋅⋅⋅⋅⋅⋅⋅⋅⋅⋅⋅⋅⋅⋅⋅⋅⋅⋅⋅⋅⋅⋅⋅⋅⋅ —

Connection to Self: Use the **H5 I Am _____ Web Diagram Skills Page** (pg. 113). Have kids write "Organized" on the blank line in the Skills Page Title. Then have kids write on the spokes the ways they can accomplish the center goal of being prepared.

Young-Thinker Activity (K-2): *Discussion.* Talk about a time when they were prepared for the day or an event. How did they feel? Next, have kids talk about a time when they weren't organized (e.g., left lunch at home, forgot homework or library book). How was this time different than the other?

In-depth Activity (3-5): *Journal writing.* Have kids write one to three paragraphs about a time when they were organized and how it made them feel. Have the kids write one to three paragraphs about a time when they weren't organized and what happened.

— ⋅⋅⋅⋅⋅⋅⋅⋅⋅⋅⋅⋅⋅⋅⋅⋅⋅⋅⋅⋅⋅⋅⋅⋅⋅⋅⋅⋅ —

Practice on Your Own: Using their **H5 I Am _____ Web Diagram Skills Page** (pg. 113), encourage kids to put a smiley face or star next to each action/spoke that they were successful in completing each day.

Theme: Do your best!

If you're good at math, you can help others with their homework before school. By encouraging others to do their best, you help build their self-confidence.

Discussion: What does it mean to do your "personal best"? (We are all different and work at different levels. When we always try to do our best, it creates self-confidence.) Have kids give two examples of when they achieved their personal best.

Compare & Contrast: Discuss what happens when we do our best and don't do our best. What are the results when you work hard and when you don't work hard? Something is missing when you aren't giving your all. What is that?

—⁙⁙⁙⁙⁙⁙⁙⁙⁙—

Connection to Self: *Journal writing.* How would you feel if you studied hard for an upcoming quiz and didn't do very well? How would getting the poor grade affect your confidence? What changes can you make for the next time? How would you feel if you had gotten a really good grade? Getting good grades keeps your confidence high.

Young-Thinker Activity (K-2): Use the **H5 Hand Skills Page** (pg. 108). This is a large-group project. Have kids name ways to do their best on the five fingers of the hand. Teacher fills out for all to see. Discuss how kids can prepare to do their best (e.g., study, practice, eat healthy, get enough rest, ask for help, etc.).

In-depth Activity (3-5): Use the **H5 Double Hand Skills Page** (pg. 102). This is an individual project. Write in the left hand those things you are good at. Write in the right hand those things that you need to work on.

—⁙⁙⁙⁙⁙⁙⁙⁙⁙—

Practice on Your Own: Teach kids this mantra that they can use whenever needed: "I feel good about myself when I do my best!"

Theme: We all make mistakes

Hey! You're smart and know how to be confident in the classroom. Raising your hand to answer a question, even if you're unsure whether your answer is correct, shows you're willing to take a chance. If you're wrong, you learn from your mistake and can try again next time.

Discussion: In a large group, discuss that everybody makes mistakes. No one knows everything. But mistakes are actually opportunities to grow and learn. Have kids talk about one scenario where they made a mistake but then learned from it and grew. Making mistakes helps build confidence.

Compare & Contrast: There are lots of different types of mistakes, but let's focus on the mistakes of our classwork and the mistakes of our behavior. Have kids complete the **H5 WWYD Skills Page** (pg. 138).

Connection to Self: *Journal writing.* Finish this sentence, "When I make a mistake in the classroom, I feel_____." Next, discuss what you would do the next time.

Young-Thinker Activity (K-2): Complete the **H5 Do's & Don'ts Word Search Skills Page** (pg. 100).

In-depth Activity (3-5): *Journal writing.* Use the following topic sentence to have kids brainstorm ways to fix the mistake: "Jessica keeps forgetting her homework" or "Pierre yells at classmates every time he can't get his way."

Practice on Your Own: Encourage kids to spend time reflecting on ways to fix a mistake they've made.

Theme: Let's work together

Hey! You're smart and know how to be confident in the classroom. Raising your hand to answer a question, even if you're unsure whether your answer is correct, shows you're willing to take a chance. If you're wrong, you learn from your mistake and can try again next time.

Discussion: What do you do when some kids don't participate in a group activity? How can you encourage all to participate?

Compare & Contrast: Discuss what happens when all members of a group work together to accomplish a goal and when only some of the members work together to accomplish a goal. How does each scenario make you feel?

Connection to Self: *Journal writing.* Have the kids answer the following: "What would you do if you were assigned to work in a group and the the kids in the group weren't your friends?" Give details how you would handle this situation.

Young-Thinker Activity (K-2): *Partner project.* To encourage kids to work together, partner kids to cut out pictures of the same theme (e.g., emotions, sports, seasons, etc.). Once their pictures are cut out, have the kids paste them on one piece of colored paper. Be sure to include the theme on the paper.

In-depth Activity (3-5): *Partner interview.* Have each student use the **H5 Who Are You? Skills Page** (pg. 135) to interview their partner. Once all questions are complete, use the **H5 Venn Diagram Skills Page** (pg. 134) to fill in their answers. Take a poll to see how many students have the most things in common.

Practice on Your Own: Partner kids and have them complete this sentence with three reasons: "Our school is the best because. . . ."

Theme: Let's solve problems

Discussion: Talk with students about what bully behavior looks like (aggressive, intentional, repetitive, and holding power over someone). Ask the students the following questions: In the first image, the short-haired girl is confronting a bully. What words might she be using? What is the boy in the background doing? Why is he there? What does the body language of the long-haired girl mean? In the second image, the long-haired girl is speaking. What words might she be using? What does the body language of the long-haired girl mean? What does the body language of the short-haired girl mean? Does it appear that the conflict is resolved?

Compare & Contrast: In the images, notice each character's body language. How is the smaller girl standing in the first image as compared to how she is standing in the second image? What are the differences in the faces of each character? Discuss the importance of body language and how we talk to each other. We want to remember to be aware of the voice tone and quality.

———⁘⁘⁘⁘⁘⁘⁘⁘⁘⁘⁘⁘⁘⁘⁘⁘⁘⁘⁘⁘⁘⁘———

Connection to Self: *Journal writing.* Talking and listening are great ways to handle conflict. Have kids name a time when they felt they handled conflict in a positive way.

Young-Thinker Activity (K-2): Have students complete the **H5 Look at My Face! Match Skills Page** (pg. 128). Explain that we know what others are feeling when we look at their face.

In-depth Activity (3-5): *Role play.* What would you do if someone pushed you out of line for the swings during recess every day? Have students brainstorm ideas for standing up to bullying behaviors and then discuss why acting like a bully is hurtful to others.

Practice on Your Own: Think about how you can help others who are being treated in a mean way.

Theme: Let's try something new

Trying something new can be very scary.
At first, you might question yourself and feel anxious.

Take a deep breath. Think positive thoughts and have courage.
Remind yourself that you can do it.

Discussion: What would happen if no one tried new things? How would that change our world? It can be scary to try new things. What one word will help a person be successful? (Courage)

Compare & Contrast: Make a list of the (perceived) positives and negatives of trying something new, such as learning to rock climb or swim, or joining a club. Can trying something new change a person's thinking?

———·⁓⋅·ℯ⋅·ⓞ⋅·ⓒ⋅·ⓞ⋅·⁓⋅·ⓞ⋅·ⓒ⋅·ⓞ⋅·ⓞ⋅·⁓⋅·ℯ⋅·ⓞ⋅·ⓒ⋅·ⓞ⋅·⁓———

Connection to Self: *Journal writing.* Have kids write one paragraph about what happened when they tried something new. How did it build their confidence? Or, did it break their confidence? If their confidence was built up, how did this experience make the student want to try something new again?

Young-Thinker Activity (K-2): Have kids research five things they would like to try. Have them rank the items 1-5 with 1 being the first thing they'd like to try. Kids should then determine how they are going to do each.

In-depth Activity (3-5): Have the kids come up with one thing they would like to try. Use the **H5 I Want to Chart Skills Page** (pg. 126) to make a plan to try something new.

———·⁓⋅·ℯ⋅·ⓞ⋅·ⓒ⋅·ⓞ⋅·⁓⋅·ⓞ⋅·ⓒ⋅·ⓞ⋅·ⓞ⋅·⁓⋅·ℯ⋅·ⓞ⋅·ⓒ⋅·ⓞ⋅·⁓———

Practice on Your Own: While at home, ask kids to find an activity that is completely new (e.g., speaking in a new language, using a yo-yo, or building a tower with cards). Have the students report back. If they like the new activity, suggest that they practice until they've mastered it. Trying new things builds self-confidence.

Theme: How do you talk to yourself?

Sometimes we think we have lost our confidence. We might say things like, "I can't do it" or "I'm dumb." Be careful! Listening to those words will make you feel bad. You won't achieve your goals using words like "I can't."

Discussion: What does it mean to say "I can't" or "I'm dumb" to yourself? How do these negative words make you feel? How do these negative words make you act?

Compare & Contrast: Using the **H5 Double Hand Skills Page** (pg. 102), fill out the left hand with how you feel when you say positive things to yourself and fill out the right hand with how you feel when you say negative things to yourself. Which hand is the best for you?

—·⌒·ℓ·⌂·◉·.◦·⌒·◉·⌒◉⌒·◦·⌒·ℓ·⌒◉·◉·◦·⌒·—

Connection to Self: *Journal writing.* Discuss a time when you used positive words to help keep your confidence. What was the situation? How did it turn out? Was it something that you did individually or in a group? Would you say any different words if you were in this situation again? Be sure to give lots of details and descriptions.

Young-Thinker Activity (K-2): Using the **H5 Hand Skills Page** (pg. 108), have kids fill in five things that they are good at doing. They can draw or write words on each finger. Discuss how being good at something relates to their levels of confidence.

In-depth Activity (3-5): *Role play.* With two or more students, have the kids act out the following scenario: One kid is saying that he/she can't do something and is using words like "I can't," "I'm afraid," "What if I look dumb?" "What if I mess up?" The other kid(s) will use positive words to help the other student develop self-confidence. Before beginning this activity, have the kids brainstorm and make a list of words that encourage others to try and do their best.

—·⌒·ℓ·⌂·◉·.◦·⌒·◉·⌒◉⌒·◦·⌒·ℓ·⌒◉·◉·◦·⌒·—

Practice on Your Own: Remind kids that when they tell themselves negative words, it makes them feel bad and can affect their behavior. Replace those words with "I will try."

Theme: Being prepared

Discussion: When have you been in a situation that made you nervous? What was it? How did you feel? What could you have done to not feel so nervous?

Compare & Contrast: Make a list of the things you would do to prepare for a math test and soccer game. Are there any similarities?

***

Connection to Self: *Journal writing.* Discuss a time when you've been involved in a group or individual activity where you had the opportunity to perform in front of people outside of school. How did you prepare? Did any previous experience help your level of confidence? Did you feel in your heart that you did your best? If you answered no to any of these questions, what could you do differently next time?

Young-Thinker Activity (K-2): *Talent show.* To help kids feel comfortable speaking in front of a group, have each student stand up and tell a knock-knock joke, sing a song, or tell a silly rhyme. Have them practice this once a month until it becomes more natural to them.

In-depth Activity (3-5): *Discussion:* Some people appear to be very confident when they have to speak in front of a group. Why do you think this happens? Discuss how the level of preparedness, past experiences, and knowing in your heart that you're going to do your best all affect a person's confidence level. How much should a person practice before speaking in front of a group? Which words do they say to themselves before speaking? What does confidence have to do with being able to speak in front of a group?

***

Practice on Your Own: At home, stand in front of the mirror and practice what you would say in front of a group. Make eye contact with yourself. How do you feel? The more you practice, the more comfortable (and confident) you'll be!

Theme: Donate your time

Donating your time at a place like an animal shelter will help the puppies and kittens be happy.

You'll feel happy, too!

Discussion: Which animals do you like? Which animals have you had experience with? How does it feel to help animals? What can you do and where can you go in your community to work with animals?

Compare & Contrast: What does it mean to be "paid" for your time? What does it mean to "donate" your time? Using these two concepts; in what types of situations would you be paid for your time and in which situations would you donate your time?

Connection to Self: *Journal writing.* Sometimes we do things for others just because we love to do them. What do you do to help others? How did you feel in your heart? Do you ever try to get a family member or friend to join you?

Young-Thinker Activity (K-2): *Service learning.* Find an animal shelter in your community and get a list of items that they need. Have each student bring something from the list to be delivered. If possible, have someone from the animal shelter bring in animals to show to the kids. The kids can then see how the animals are so grateful for their new toys/treats/etc.

In-depth Activity (3-5): Search YouTube for an interview with a volunteer. You can find one here with a dentist who volunteers in Nepal: www.youtube.com/watch?v=RusCruQuXQ4. Have kids watch the video and then write a three-paragraph essay using the following: (1) Where did the video take place and what did the volunteer do? (2) What did the volunteer gain from his experience and what did the people gain from his volunteering? (3) What you would like to volunteer for?

Practice on Your Own: *Service learning.* Find an opportunity in your community to give of yourself (time, talents, and energy) and make a habit of participating. Invite a friend or a family member to go with you.

Theme: Working hard in your community (service learning)

Raking leaves can be hard work, but you're willing to help someone who can't do the job. Confident people don't mind stepping up to do hard work.

Discussion: What does hard work mean to you? Is it physical or mental? Sometimes when it's a big project, many people have to be involved to get the job done. People don't mind working hard to achieve a goal. What goal would you like to work toward?

Compare & Contrast: Research two charitable organizations. Use the **H5 Venn Diagram Skills Page** (pg. 134) to show the differences and similarities.

Connection to Self: *Journal writing.* When we help others, we feel as much joy in giving as they do in receiving. Describe a time when you were able to make a difference in someone's life. Did you feel it was a win-win? If yes, describe how both parties won.

Young-Thinker Activity (K-2): *Service learning.* Have students do an easy service-learning project such as cleaning up the playground, collecting cans for local food pantry, organizing a can and bottle drive for monies to be donated to a local charity, etc.

In-depth Activity (3-5): When we reach out beyond ourselves, we are helping human rights. View the Habitat for Humanity "Why We Build" video www.youtube.com/watch?v=OE6Rg7xhTrQ and have students write a three-paragraph essay using the following: (1) Where did the video take place and what do the volunteers do? (2) What is gained by the people who benefit from Habitat for Humanity? (3) If you could volunteer for Habitat for Humanity, what would you do?

Practice on Your Own: Invite a community organization leader (i.e., Rotary, Kiwanis, Lions, etc.) into the classroom to talk about their volunteer/charitable activities. On their own, have students prepare questions to interview the guest speaker.

Theme: Being a true friend

When someone is trustworthy, honest, and caring, you can rely on them to be a true friend.

Discussion: What does it mean to be trustworthy? What does it mean to be a true friend (not lying, not gossiping about others, being caring, being a good listener, etc.)? How can you show that you are a true friend?

Compare & Contrast: Use the **H5 Venn Diagram Skills Page** (pg. 134) to compare and contrast the two characters of a book such as *Being Friends* by Karen Beaumont.

Connection to Self: *Journal writing.* Discuss a time when you acted like a true friend or when someone else acted as a true friend toward you. Describe what happened and how you felt.

Young-Thinker Activity (K-2): Complete the **H5 True Friend Word Search Skills Page** (pg. 132). Discuss any words that may be new to the students.

In-depth Activity (3-5): After studying this picture, ask the students who has more trust: the boy in the wheelchair or the boy pushing the wheelchair. The boy trusts the pusher and the boy pushing trusts himself that he's able to push uphill. Have students complete the **H5 C-O-N-F-I-D-E-N-T Acrostic Skills Page** (pg. 96). Use the **H5 C-O-N-F-I-D-E-N-T Acrostic Word List Skills Page** (pg. 97) for help. Discuss the words for each letter.

Practice on Your Own: Use this mantra: "I'm a helpful kid who cares!"

Theme: What it takes to be a good leader

A strong leader is also a confident person. When you are chosen to be the captain or leader of your team, be a good role model for the other team members.

Discussion: What does it mean to be a positive role model? Name a positive role model in your life. Is it a sister, teacher, parent, coach, friend?

Compare & Contrast: Using the **H5 T-Chart Skills Page** (pg. 131), have the kids work in groups to determine the characteristics of a positive role model. Write "Positive Role Model" on the right side and "Negative Role Model" on the left side. Note the similarities and differences between the two lists.

———————

Connection to Self: *Journal writing.* Let's pretend you're the leader of a group of three kids and everyone has been given a part to do for a classroom project. When the group meets, you find out that the three kids haven't done their work. What would you do?

Young-Thinker Activity (K-2): *Discussion.* If someone left a game because their feelings were hurt, what would you do to get them to come back to the game?

In-depth Activity (3-5): *Role play.* Have groups of four kids role play the following: A teammate is having trouble scoring a goal. How would you encourage that person?

———————

Practice on Your Own: Invite a local positive role model (e.g., a coach) to speak to the kids about encouragement. Have the kids come up with one question each about how the speaker learned to be a good leader.

Theme: Nobody's perfect

Discussion: Have students look up the word "perfect" in the dictionary and write it out so all can see. Discuss what it means to be perfect in relation to the definition. Is it possible for a person to be perfect? Is it possible for a person to do perfect things (e.g., get a 100% on a test)? Does getting 100% mean a person is perfect? Remember to always refer to the definition because NO ONE is perfect.

Compare & Contrast: List the skills needed for baseball and the skills needed for basketball. Discuss the similarities and differences of how to become a good player in each sport.

Connection to Self: *Journal writing.* Have you ever felt like you were perfect at something and could do no wrong? Were you really perfect? Name three things that helped you get good at something.

Young-Thinker Activity (K-2): Use the **H5 Double Hand Skills Page** (pg. 102). Have kids write about or draw pictures of what they are good at on the left hand. On the right hand, have kids write about or draw pictures of what they would like to become better at. Discuss ways for those things on the right hand to move over to the left hand (practice).

In-depth Activity (3-5): Does a confident person who excels at something (e.g., sport, academics, etc.) appear to be perfect? Does being confident mean that you can be perfect? Have kids research a sports hero or someone who has excelled in a particular area. Have kids determine if the word "perfect" is ever used to describe this person.

Practice on Your Own: Focus on a new interest and encourage practicing to build self-confidence.

Theme: How can you show others support?

Putting others down is not how a confident person behaves. Remember to be supportive when someone makes mistakes.

Discussion: Discuss what it means to show support to others (e.g., being a good listener, giving encouragement, not putting others down, using kind words, etc.). Brainstorm ten situations where kids can show support to others.

Compare & Contrast: How can you show support to someone verbally and physically? List ways for both.

Connection to Self: *Journal writing.* Have you ever felt put down because you made a mistake? Describe the situation.

Young-Thinker Activity (K-2): Role play the perspectives and feelings of the following characters: the baseball player as he walks past his teammates and the two teammates. What words do the teammates use to encourage the player who struck out? What words does the player who made the mistake use?

In-depth Activity (3-5): Have kids complete the **H5 Who Has Excellent Character? ME!! Word Search Skills Page** (pg. 136).

Practice on Your Own: Interview a person (i.e., friend, parent, neighbor, etc.) who encourages others. Ask them why they think it's important to encourage others

Respect

How can I teach respectfulness today?

Thank you for putting your best foot forward to build respectful children. Teachers tell us constantly that the reason they go into teaching is to make a difference. We want a balance between academics and character. That balance will empower kids to be wonderful people. Our task is great but worth the effort. We know that is takes a village, so we willingly take the steps to develop confidence and respect each and every day.

This section is designed to reinforce respect and show kids how respect occurs in every aspect of our lives. We don't practice respect for just a few minutes a day; it becomes part of our heart, our behavior, and our life.

Respect is a skill that will carry every person through any experience that each has to deal with in life. Put respect at the top of your list!

Words and phrases that you can use in your classroom:
- "Look for the good in each other."
- "Be sincere when apologizing."
- "Each person is responsible for his/her own behavior."
- "No blaming."
- "Patience, patience."
- "Practice and never give up."

Encourage healthy body language:
- Look at the student's face
- Speak from your heart
- Show considerate behavior to others

TUESDAY is all about being RESPECTFUL!

Theme: Bring on the respect!

Read this book before you begin.

Find the definition of the character trait (respect).
Have the kids name five ways to be respectful as shown in the book. Post answers for all to see.

Try This!
Have all kids repeat the mantra on this page five times out loud: **"I'm going to be kind to everyone."**

Character question: How do they feel after repeating the mantra? This mantra is to help kids feel empowered to do their best. Teachers can encourage kids that each should be doing their best all day.

End of Day Character Challenge: What was the mantra they said in the morning? "I'm going to be kind to everyone." Give high-fives to all students.

Theme: How can we show respect to our parents and others?

Your dad may help you get your lunch ready or check your homework. It's important to him to make sure you're ready for school. You look up to your dad which shows you respect him.

"Thanks, Dad!"

Discussion: Why do we need to show respect to your parents, caregivers, and others? Before you go to school in the morning, name four things that your parent/caregiver does for you.

Compare & Contrast: Brainstorm ways to be respectful at home and in school. What are the differences and similarities between the two situations?

Connection to Self: *Journal writing.* Parents and caregivers raise their children with love and kindness and deserve to be treated the same. Name three ways you can show respect to your parent/caregiver.

Young-Thinker Activity (K-2): Complete the **H5 I Am Respectful Word Search Skills Page** (pg. 122). Discuss words that may be new to students.

In-depth Activity (3-5): *Journal writing.* Have students use the following starter sentence to write one paragraph that shows five ways they are respectful toward their parents/caregivers every day: "I show respect to my parents/caregiver by..."

Practice on Your Own: Make a list of ways you can show respect to your parents/caregiver and hang it on your refrigerator or someplace where you'll see it every day.

Theme: Open your ears and listen!

Your sister shows respect for you by listening to you sing a song you learned at school.

Discussion: How do you act when you are listening to someone? Why is it important to listen carefully? When you are actively listening to another person, you are being respectful to that person.

Compare & Contrast: Using the **H5 T-Chart Skills Page** (pg. 131), compare and contrast a person who is actively listening and a person who is not listening. Be sure to include body language.

—⟶⟶

Connection to Self: *Journal writing.* Name a situation when you weren't listening. What were the results?

Young-Thinker Activity (K-2): Use the **H5 I Am _____ Web Diagram Skills Page** (pg. 113). Have kids write "A Good Listener" on the line in the Skills Page title. In the center circle, have students write their names. On the outer spokes, have the kids list ways to be a good listener. They can either write words or draw pictures.

In-depth Activity (3-5): *Persuasive writing.* Write a persuasive essay on this topic: What would happen in your home, school, community, state, country, etc., if no one listened to anybody?

—⟶⟶

Practice on Your Own: Find a situation at school, at home, or in a group activity where you can practice being an active listener.

Theme: Being careful with others' belongings

By playing carefully with your cousin's toys, you show respect for her.

Discussion: Why is it important to be careful with others' belongings and what does this have to do with respect? Is it true that if you respect the person you'll respect their belongings?

Compare & Contrast: How does a respectful person play with others' toys? How does a disrespectful person play with others' toys? Are there any similarities or differences?

———— ·ᘓ·ᐤ·ᐤ·ᐤ·ᐤ·ᐤ·ᐤ·ᐤ·ᐤ·ᐤ·ᐤ·ᐤ·ᐤ·ᐤ·ᐤ·ᐤ·ᐤ·ᐤ ————

Connection to Self: *Journal writing.* What would you do if someone was playing with your toy and broke it? What would you do if you wanted to play with a toy but your friend wouldn't share?

Young-Thinker Activity (K-2): *Partner project.* Pair kids and have one ask the other if he/she can play with that person's favorite toy. The answer should be "yes" but the student should also explain how to play with the toy carefully. Reverse the roles.

In-depth Activity (3-5): Create a three-step plan for solving the problem of breaking a friend's toy. You can use the **H5 3-Box Sequence Strip** (pg. 90) and include pictures and words or students can write out the plan.

———— ·ᘓ·ᐤ·ᐤ·ᐤ·ᐤ·ᐤ·ᐤ·ᐤ·ᐤ·ᐤ·ᐤ·ᐤ·ᐤ·ᐤ·ᐤ·ᐤ·ᐤ·ᐤ ————

Practice on Your Own: Remind yourself often, "I'm respectful to others when I'm respectful of their belongings."

Theme: Paying attention shows a lot to others

Discussion: Respectful people understand and follow the rules. Describe consequences for breaking classroom rules. Should there be rules in the classroom? Why?

Compare & Contrast: Body language is how we communicate without words. Have kids partner for this activity. One child should show how to be respectful without using words. The other child should show how to NOT be respectful without using words. Students should discuss how they felt. Afterward, have students switch roles and repeat.

Connection to Self: Using the **H5 Becoming a Better Me! Chart Skills Page** (pg. 93), have kids fill out the left side with times that they show respect consistently. Fill out the right side with times that they need help showing respect (e.g., waiting for the swing during recess, standing quietly in line, etc.).

Young-Thinker Activity (K-2): Have kids make a list of respectful behavior that is shown in the image. Who is showing respect?

In-depth Activity (3-5): *Journal writing.* Discuss what would happen if we didn't have rules in school, at home, or in the community.

Practice on Your Own: During the day, pay attention to when you aren't being respectful.

Theme: Hey...shhh!

You can be respectful of your classmates by using a quiet voice during library time.

Discussion: What's happening in this image? What are some ways to handle conflict like this? What would happen if one of the characters started shoving or yelling? Would the conflict be resolved?

Compare & Contrast: Look at the faces of the two girls and the boy sitting on the stool. How would you describe how they are reacting? Now look at the faces of the boy with glasses and the boy in the plaid shirt. How are they feeling? What are the similarities and differences between the two groups?

Connection to Self: *Journal writing.* Have you ever been the boy in the plaid shirt? How did you handle the situation?

Young-Thinker Activity (K-2): Name three places you need to be quiet.

In-depth Activity (3-5): *Partner project.* Problem solve the best ways to handle a situation like the one shown in the image. Come together as a class and share the students' ideas.

Practice on Your Own: Practice being aware of wanting to talk in situations when you should be quiet.

Theme: Taking your turn

When you're having fun, waiting for your turn can be difficult.

Being patient shows respect for others.

Discussion: What does it mean to be patient? Why is it important to be patient? Why is it important to take turns?

Compare & Contrast: Make a list of how a patient person acts and how an impatient person acts. Are there any differences? Similarities? Which is the more respectful way to act?

—·◦᠅ ℓ ⊙ ◎·. ◦ ᠅ᢀ ·⊙ ◎ ◎·. ◉·᠅ᢀ ℓ ·◎᠅ ◉ ᢀ ᠅ᢀ·—

Connection to Self: *Journal writing.* Write about a time you had to be patient. How did you feel? Was it hard to be patient?

Young-Thinker Activity (K-2): Sometimes it's hard to wait your turn. Have kids complete the **H5 I Am a Patient Kid Skills Page** (pg. 116) to help reinforce being patient.

In-depth Activity (3-5): *Partner project.* Brainstorm steps to be patient in the following situations: waiting to open birthday gifts, waiting in a long line for ice cream, waiting for a ride on a roller coaster.

—·◦᠅ ℓ ⊙ ◎·. ◦ ᠅ᢀ ·⊙ ◎ ◎·. ◉·᠅ᢀ ℓ ·◎᠅ ◉ ᢀ ᠅ᢀ·—

Practice on Your Own: Encourage kids to look for others being patient. Provide **H5 High 5ver!** (pg. 109) forms so that kids can acknowledge the efforts of others. Read the **H5 High 5ver!** forms and give high-fives to the kids who are being acknowledged.

Theme: Following directions

Your coach or leader will know you are respectful when you listen and pay attention to details.

Discussion: What are the characters in this image doing? Why are they doing this? Notice that everyone is pitching in to help and working together to make this area look nice.

Compare & Contrast: What would a classroom look like if no one followed directions? What does a classroom look like when everyone follows directions? Are there any similarities or differences between these two classrooms?

Connection to Self: What is a service project? Make a list of service projects in your community that clean up the earth. Name three service projects that you can do to help people.

Young-Thinker Activity (K-2): Have students draw a picture of how they followed directions either at home or at an extra-curricular activity. What happens when they don't follow directions?

In-depth Activity (3-5): Make a list of when people need to follow directions at home, at school, in the community, when playing a sport, or when participating in a group. Is life easier when we all follow directions? Why or why not? How does the leader help a group succeed?

Practice on Your Own: Research a favorite recipe online. Print it out and make it at home with a trusted adult.

Theme: How do you treat yourself?

Discussion: Why is it important to use positive words when we talk to ourselves? How do we feel when we say, "I can't do it!"? What if you said, "I'll try"?

Compare & Contrast: Complete the **H5 Who Has Excellent Character? ME!! Word Search Skills Page** (pg. 136).

——·⫯⸋⫯⸋⫯⸋⸋⫯⸋⸋⫯⸋⸋——

Connection to Self: *Journal writing.* How do you keep healthy? How are eating right and exercising good ways to show yourself respect?

Young-Thinker Activity (K-2): Have kids draw pictures of what a healthy person eats.

In-depth Activity (3-5): *Health sciences.* Help kids determine their resting heart rate. Use the tips of your first two fingers and press lightly over the blood vessels on the inside of your wrist, thumb side. Count your heartbeats for 10 seconds and then multiply by 6. This number is your resting heart rate in beats per minute. According to the National Institute of Health, the average resting heart rate for kids 10 years and older and adults is 60-100 beats per minute. According to the American Heart Association, when you exercise your heart rate should be between 50% and 85% of your maximum heart rate. The Mayo Clinic states to figure your maximum heart rate, subtract your age from 220, then multiply that number by 50%. That would be the lowest maximum heart rate you should have when exercising intensely. What are your resting and lowest maximum heart rates?

——·⫯⸋⫯⸋⫯⸋⸋⫯⸋⸋⫯⸋⸋——

Practice on Your Own: Make a journal of what you eat or how much you exercise for one week.

Theme: How do you solve problems?

Sometimes we forget to be respectful. You might say something rude to your friend, brother, or sister. Be sure to apologize for acting that way and make sure it doesn't happen again.

"I'm really sorry."

Discussion: How do you feel when someone is not respectful toward you? Do you feel better after they apologize? What can you do so you don't forget to be respectful to others?

Compare & Contrast: In the picture, one girl is doing the talking while the other is listening. When you say "I am sorry" and you mean it, is that respectful? What if you don't really mean it? Are you telling a lie? Is that fair? Do you think others can tell when you are lying?

Connection to Self: Watch the video "What Does Respect Mean To You?" http://youtu.be/i1B0af825U4 and then have the students list words of what respect means to them.

Young-Thinker Activity (K-2): Discuss with the students a time when they felt the same way as the characters do in the above image. Have kids complete the **H5 How I Feel Skills Page** (pg. 112) to identify positive and negative feelings/faces.

In-depth Activity (3-5): *Journal writing.* Analyze the consequences of lying. Respectful people are honest.

- Why should we tell the truth?
- Does each of us show respect for ourselves and others if we lie?
- Can others trust us if we lie?
- Will others want to play with us if we lie?
- What do we need to change in order to have respect from others?

Practice on Your Own: Some kids have a harder time saying the words "I'm really sorry." Have kids practice saying these words to themselves in a mirror.

Theme: Spending time with grandparents and other family members

Show your grandparents that you appreciate them by treating them respectfully. Always look for the good in each other.

Discussion: Why is it important to spend time with family members? What activities do you do when you're with your family? What makes those activities so important?

Compare & Contrast: Pick two activities that you do with a family member. What is different about the two activities? What is the same?

—·⁓ ℮ ⊙ ⊙ ᦒ ·₀ ⁓ꞏ ⊙ ⊙ ℮ꞏ ⊙ꞏ⁓ ℮ ⊙ ⊙ ₀ ⁓—

Connection to Self: Have students bring in pictures of when they were young, such as two or three years old. Ask the following questions:
- Do you remember when you were little? When you were little, could you ride a bike, run fast, play a sport, or read a book?
- What could you do when you were that age?
- How did each thing that you learned help you become a better person today?
- Who taught you how to do things like eat with silverware, walk and run, kick a ball, and read?

Young-Thinker Activity (K-2): Complete the **H5 I Care! Word Search Skills Page** (pg. 124).

In-depth Activity (3-5): Use the **H5 I Am _____ Web Diagram Skills Page** (pg. 113). Have kids write "A Good Role Model" on the blank line in the Skills Page Title. Choose a family member and write that person's name in the center circle or draw a picture of the person. On the spokes, write what makes this person so special to you. Finally, answer: Why did you pick this person?

—·⁓ ℮ ⊙ ⊙ ᦒ ·₀ ⁓ꞏ ⊙ ⊙ ℮ꞏ ⊙ꞏ⁓ ℮ ⊙ ⊙ ₀ ⁓—

Practice on Your Own: Write a note to a family member telling why that person is special to you.

Theme: Family events

Every time you go to a friend's soccer game or your sister's dance recital, you're being respectful of them.

Great job!

Discussion: Why are special events important? What do you do if you think the event isn't special? How do you act?

Compare & Contrast: What are respectful behaviors at a soccer game and a dance recital? Use the **H5 Venn Diagram Skills Page** (pg. 134) to show the similarities and the differences. For example, is yelling positive words at a dance recital appropriate behavior or is that more for a soccer game?

—

Connection to Self: What is a compliment? Saying kind words to others is being respectful. Notice in the picture it says, "Great job!" Are these words for adults or children to use? Have students make a list of kind words that can be used when giving a compliment.

Young-Thinker Activity (K-2): Have students draw a picture of how they are respectful when they are at a friend's or family member's special event. Be sure to include the name of the event (e.g., Nick's hockey game).

In-depth Activity (3-5): Have students complete the **H5 R-E-S-P-E-C-T Acrostic Skills Page** (pg. 129). Use the **H5 R-E-S-P-E-C-T Acrostic Word List Skills Page** (pg. 130) for help. Discuss the words for each letter.

—

Practice on Your Own: Before you go home today, give two people compliments.

Theme: Taking responsibility for your behavior

If you treat others with respect, most times they'll treat you the same. To get respect, you have to give respect. It's easy! When everyone takes responsibility for their own behavior, we are respectful people.

Discussion: Why is it important for each person to take responsibility for his/her behavior?

Compare & Contrast: Compare this page with the first page of "How we treat each other" on page 40. Which boy is showing respect on each page? Which boy isn't showing respect?

Connection to Self: *Small-group discussion.* What would you do if you had a friend who always blamed everything on someone else?

Young-Thinker Activity (K-2): *Role play.* Have one child act as the honored adult and another as the child wanting to shake hands. Who is showing respect?

In-depth Activity (3-5): *Journal writing.* Describe in detail a situation when you took responsibility for your own behavior. It could be that you did your chores, apologized for being rude, or another situation. Did taking responsibility change the way you acted in the future?

Practice on Your Own: Practice the following chant: "I'm at my best when I respect at home or at school. I do my best when I respect."

Theme: Taking care of the environment

We need to be respectful of our environment and other people's property. Don't litter, always recycle, and be careful with items that don't belong to you.

Discussion: Why is it important to take care of the environment? Watch this short video from National Geographic, "Why Care about Water?" http://video.nationalgeographic.com/video/env-freshwater-whycare and then discuss ways kids can conserve water.

Compare & Contrast: What are the best ways we are preserving our water and trees? What are the pros and cons of each? Do research online or check local activities.

Connection to Self: *Journal writing.* If you could clean up the world, how would you do it?

Young-Thinker Activity (K-2): What parts of the environment can we respect? (You are looking for words like "water," "flowers," "air," "forests," etc.) What animals can we respect and how? Have students name some of the ways they have respected their world. To reinforce respect of things in nature, have students complete the **H5 Clean and Tidy Word Search Skills Page** (pg. 94).

In-depth Activity (3-5): Make a list of four things in our environment that we need to care for. Choose one and write about how we can preserve it. This can be done individually or in groups. If done in groups, have each group present to the class and have them create campaign posters to show their support for their project.

Practice on Your Own: Organize a neighborhood clean-up.

Theme: How we treat each other

Discussion: What does it mean to "judge" a person in a disrespectful way? What words could you use or actions you could take if your friend was judging someone else?

Compare & Contrast: Look at the two images above. Compare the text that is happening in the first image to the text that is happening in the second image. Which do you think shows more respect, text from image #1 or image #2?

———·⁓♪ ℓ ☽ ◎ ☾ ⚬ ⁓♪·☾ ◎ ⚬☾ ◎ ☾·◎·⁓♪ ℓ ⚬☽ ◎ ⚬ ☾⚬·———

Connection to Self: *Partner interview.* Has a friend ever said something mean about someone else based on how they looked or acted? What did you do? If you acted in a mean way, how could you have acted differently?

Young-Thinker Activity (K-2): Use the **H5 Venn Diagram Skills Page** (pg. 134) to show the similarities and differences of each picture. Have kids use words or draw pictures.

In-depth Activity (3-5): In the image above, two boys have to make a decision. Should they let peer pressure make them act in a mean way? Did the boys listen to the one who was saying mean things? How did the boys support the one in the wheelchair? Look at the face of the boy in the wheelchair. How do you think he feels about his friends supporting him? What is the right thing to do in other situations when people are being mean and critical of others?

———·⁓♪ ℓ ☽ ◎ ☾ ⚬ ⁓♪·☾ ◎ ⚬☾ ◎ ☾·◎·⁓♪ ℓ ⚬☽ ◎ ⚬ ☾⚬·———

Practice on Your Own: Repeat this: "Look for the likenesses and not the differences."

Empathy

How can I teach empathy today?

Thank you for believing in the High 5 for Character Program.

You might think it is difficult to teach empathy, but really it is not. It is all about the heart. When we have caring in our hearts, we have empathy. We show others we care by how we treat them.

As adults, it is our job to introduce empathy, reinforce it, and teach kids how to treat each other. It can be done by modeling the behavior and can also be done by embedding in their minds the correct words in the correct situations. If kids know what to say and they feel it in their hearts, they will respond in the correct manner.

Words and phrases that you can use in your classroom:
- "I care."
- "Are you okay?"
- "Can I help?"
- "I feel sad."

Encourage healthy body language:
- Be attentive
- Use eye contact
- Listen carefully
- Smile
- Be aware of others around you

WEDNESDAY is all about being EMPATHETIC!

Theme: Bring on the empathy!

Read this book before you begin.

Find the definition of the character trait (empathy).
Have the kids name five ways to be empathetic as shown in the book. Post answers for all to see.

Try This!
Have all kids repeat the mantra on this page five times out loud: **"I am going to be aware of how others feel."**

Character question: How do they feel after repeating the mantra? This mantra is to help kids feel empowered to do their best. Teachers can encourage kids that each should be doing their best all day.

End of Day Character Challenge: What was the mantra they said in the morning? "I am going to be aware of how others feel." Give high-fives to all students.

Theme: Helping family members and others

Helping your brother do his chores makes the job easier for him and takes less time. Noticing that he needs help is showing empathy.

"Thanks!"

Discussion: Name a time when you helped someone in your family without being asked. How did they respond?

Compare & Contrast: Have students choose an activity that they can do at home and compare the time it would take to complete with help and without help. This could be as simple as folding clothes, taking out the trash, or cleaning your room.

—❦❦❦❦❦❦❦❦❦❦❦❦❦❦❦❦❦❦—

Connection to Self: *Partner interview.* What would you do if you had to do all of the chores at home by yourself? Would it seem like a lot of work? What could make the job easier?

Young-Thinker Activity (K-2): Have students create a "Chore Coupon" that promises to do a specific chore at home and have them give the coupon to a family member. Encourage students to report back how that person felt after the student completed the chore.

In-depth Activity (3-5): *Argumentative writing.* Write an argumentative paragraph: Should siblings help each other do chores? Write a persuasive paragraph that will convince your friends why you are showing empathy when you help others, especially without being asked.

—❦❦❦❦❦❦❦❦❦❦❦❦❦❦❦❦❦❦—

Practice on Your Own: Find a person a day to help. It could be in school, at home, or in the community or sports. It can be as simple as holding the door open for someone or putting the balls away after practice.

Theme: Listening to a friend

A friend tells you that he lost his pet.
Even if this hasn't happened to you,
you know how sad he feels just by looking at his face.
You feel bad for him.

Discussion: Have you ever felt sad and needed to talk to somebody? When a person is having a difficult time, he or she may need to talk about what is happening. An empathetic person will volunteer to listen and be supportive. You don't need to solve the problem, but just listen. A trusted friend will listen and care.

Compare & Contrast: Using the **H5 T-Chart Skills Page** (pg. 131), write "Being a Good Listener" on the left side and write "Not Listening" on the right side. List words/ actions for each category. Are there any similarities?

—⁓⦾⦿⦾⦿⦾⦾⦾⦾⦿⦾⦿⦾⦾⦿⦾⦿⦾⦾⦾⦾⦿⦾⦿⦾⦾—

Connection to Self: *Role play.* What would you do if you saw someone crying on the bus? What would you do if you saw someone with their knee bleeding? What would you do if a friend was sad because he/she had to move?

Young-Thinker Activity (K-2): Have kids fill out the **H5 How I Feel Skills Page** (pg. 112). Once completed, role play how each child would act when they saw a friend with each feeling.

In-depth Activity (3-5): Have students come up with a situation where they knew someone who was hurting or upset about something. Then, write a letter to the person who was sad or hurting.

—⁓⦾⦿⦾⦿⦾⦾⦾⦾⦿⦾⦿⦾⦾⦿⦾⦿⦾⦾⦾⦾⦿⦾⦿⦾⦾—

Practice on Your Own: Practice looking at others' faces to see their emotions. Look at your mom or dad's face, teacher's face, bus driver's face, or coach's face. What are you seeing? Practice smiling at everyone you see.

Theme: Helping another person

When the librarian has a cart full of books, you and your friend give her a helping hand.

Discussion: Why is teamwork important? What are some activities that require teamwork?

Compare & Contrast: Have a student pick up a number of books or supplies and ask him/her to open the door on their own. Notice how hard it is to manage moving from one place to another by yourself with an armful of books. Now do the same thing but have someone help with the door. Discuss the differences.

—⋅⟡⋅⟡⋅⟡⋅⟡⋅⟡⋅⟡⋅⟡⋅⟡⋅⟡⋅⟡⋅⟡⋅⟡—

Connection to Self: *Small-group discussion.* Think of a time when you needed help. Did you ask someone to help you or did they offer? Reminder: asking in a nice way gets a quicker response.

Young-Thinker Activity (K-2): Using the **H5 3-Box Sequence Strip Skills Page** (pg. 90), draw pictures of a situation when you helped a teacher, librarian, or lunch person. The first box should be the beginning, the second box should be the middle, and the third box should be the end.

In-depth Activity (3-5): How did they build the pyramids? They did not have cranes or forklifts back then. It was by manpower. People helping people. Complete the **H5 5 Ways to Lend a Hand Skills Page** (pg. 91).

—⋅⟡⋅⟡⋅⟡⋅⟡⋅⟡⋅⟡⋅⟡⋅⟡⋅⟡⋅⟡⋅⟡⋅⟡—

Practice on Your Own: Practice asking people around you if they need help. Practice saying things like "I can help you" or "Do you need help?" or "Let me help you." Tell your friends to do the same and compare notes on what you did and how others responded. It feels great to lend a hand.

Theme: Asking for help to improve your grades

Discussion: Who should you turn to when you need help with your subjects in school? You might turn to your parent or another student in your class. It can be embarrassing to ask for help, especially if you get a poor grade on a paper. Should you just give up or try to fix it? What if you turned to your teacher?

Compare & Contrast: You study but there might be some tips that a teacher can offer to help you do better next time. Compare a time when you got help with a time when you didn't. How did you do on your test in each situation?

Connection to Self: Ask your teacher to give you tips to improve your grade. Your teacher wants the best for you as well (that's empathy), but you need to go to him/her and ask if there is anything you can do to get a better grade. Remember: your grades are your responsibility, so take action!

Young-Thinker Activity (K-2): Use the **H5 I Am _____ Web Diagram Skills Page** (pg. 113) to help kids get ready to study. Have kids write "Ready to Study" on the blank line in the Skills Page Title. What do you need to be prepared? Name five things that you need to study.

In-depth Activity (3-5): Use the **H5 I Want To ... Chart Skills Page** (pg. 126) to plan your study time each day. The more you practice, the more prepared you will be. Stick to your chart each day. If you do not understand the lesson, then go to your teacher and ask for help to have one-on-one time with that person.

Practice on Your Own: Share your study ideas from the **In-depth Activity** with friends.

Theme: Being in a new situation

Discussion: Have you ever been the new kid in a new school or in any group? Being the new kid can really create a lot of fear, anxiety, and worry. Discuss with your class what it is like to be the new kid.

Compare & Contrast: *Partner project.* Have each student complete the **H5 Who Are You Skills Page** (pg. 135). Star the answers that are the same on both sheets.

Connection to Self: How would you like others to treat you? You want others to accept you for who you are and not judge you by your clothes, your looks, or how you talk. Invite someone you don't know really well to play at recess or sit by you at lunch.

Young-Thinker Activity (K-2): Have the group make a list of five ways to act kind to someone they don't know in their class.

In-depth Activity (3-5): *Journal writing.* When a new kid comes to your school, they may be shy, lonely, frightened, and worried about whether they will fit in. Sometimes kids act tough because they are afraid that if they don't act tough, they will be treated in a mean way. Have students write about how they would act as a new student in school or on a team. When everyone is finished, ask students to read what they wrote.

Practice on Your Own: Smile at ten people today.

Theme: How can you help a hurt or injured friend?

You can help your friend with his lunch because you know how hard it is to get around when you have an injury.

"Thanks, dude!"

"No problem!"

Discussion: Many people have had a broken leg, arm, or wrist and needed help to get around. Are you the kind of person who will reach out and help someone in need? What can you deduce from the boys' smiles on this page?

Compare & Contrast: How can a person who has an injury manage to get around on their own? Compare this boy on crutches who doesn't have his hands free to someone who has a broken arm. How would helping them be different?

—⁓⁓⁓⁓⁓⁓⁓⁓⁓⁓⁓⁓—

Connection to Self: *Journal writing.* Imagine you are injured. Think of five ways you would ask for help and five ways you would respond to someone who offers to help without being asked.

Young-Thinker Activity (K-2): *Role play.* Have two students act out this page (one is hurt and one is helping). What words does each use to show empathy and gratitude?

In-depth Activity (3-5): Use the **H5 E-M-P-A-T-H-Y Acrostic Skills Page** (pg. 103) to develop empathetic thinking. If kids need help, use the **H5 E-M-P-A-T-H-Y Acrostic Word List Skills Page** (pg. 104). Have students write their words and then share them with the class to see words that others might use. It is good to post the words under each letter on the white board or an empathy bulletin board.

—⁓⁓⁓⁓⁓⁓⁓⁓⁓⁓⁓⁓—

Practice on Your Own: Throughout the school year, be aware of others who may be hurt and need help.

Theme: How to make a difference in someone's life

Sometimes helping out can be difficult, but it's worth it when you can make a difference for someone.

Wow! You really care!

Discussion: Why should you help someone if it may be difficult for you? You may have to be available to lift or carry things. You may have to be available to that person and put them first.

Compare & Contrast: Compare how you would help the following people whether they are injured or not: an elderly person (like Grandma/Grandpa), a small child, a person in a wheelchair, a baby, and a blind person. Would you treat any of these people differently?

—⋅◦◦⋅ℯ⋅⊙ ⊙◦⋅◦ ◦◦ ⋅◦⋅◦⋅⊙ ⋅◦◦ ◦◦⋅ ◦⋅◦◦ℯ⋅◦ ⋅◦◦ ⊙⋅◦ ◦◦ —

Connection to Self: Imagine you have received help because you're injured. You know what it is like to feel relieved when someone offers to carry your books or science project to class. Name two ways you can show them that you appreciate the empathy they have shown you. This cannot include giving them money.

Young-Thinker Activity (K-2): Using the **H5 I'm a Helper Word Search Skills Page** (pg. 114), have students work on this individually or in small groups. Then have students give examples of when they have been helpful to others.

In-depth Activity (3-5): *Journal writing.* Have kids write a paragraph answering the following question: What would you do if you saw your mom struggling to carry all of the grocery bags? If you don't help her, look at her face and describe how she feels. If you do help her, look at her face and describe how she feels.

—⋅◦◦⋅ℯ⋅⊙ ⊙◦⋅◦ ◦◦ ⋅◦⋅◦⋅⊙ ⋅◦◦ ◦◦⋅ ◦⋅◦◦ℯ⋅◦ ⋅◦◦ ⊙⋅◦ ◦◦ —

Practice on Your Own: Practice putting another person first every day, even if only for a few minutes. Look at the response you get when you act in a kind and caring manner. Write down what you did and how that person responded. Then tell another person what happened and encourage them to do the same.

Theme: Think before you speak and act

Discussion: How can words hurt other people's feelings?

Compare & Contrast: What are the differences and similarities in these pages? How do the kids look different on the page on the left and how do they look the same on the right? Notice the teasing, but also notice how others come forward to defend. In the end, we are more alike than different.

———— ✦✧ ✧ ◌ ◉ ﹒ ✧ ◉ ◉ ◉ ◉ ◉ ﹒ ✧✧ ✧ ◉ ◉ ◌ ✧ ————

Connection to Self: Have you ever had braces or new glasses? Did you feel self-conscious at first? What was your biggest fear? Finish this sentence: I think kids can stop teasing by _____.

Young-Thinker Activity (K-2): Find the video "How to Unmake a Bully" https://www.youtube.com/watch?v=N0f6qQrvD8k and scroll to 12:40 and watch until 14:10. Notice how the boys tease him. Look at Harold's face and see how he feels. Take a vote in the class and decide as a group if they would tease or be kind to Harold. Make a list of kind words to say to others instead of teasing.

In-depth Activity (3-5): Use the **H5 3-Box Sequence Strip Skills Page** (pg. 90) and have students draw a 3-part scene that shows a time when someone said hurtful things to them or they witnessed this. What happened? Then have kids show their scenes to the class and tell what the right thing to do is and why empathy is important.

———— ✦✧ ✧ ◌ ◉ ﹒ ✧ ◉ ◉ ◉ ◉ ◉ ﹒ ✧✧ ✧ ◉ ◉ ◌ ✧ ————

Practice on Your Own: In the picture on the left, notice that there are bystanders who are watching. What do the bystanders do in the second picture? Think of three things you can do, as a bystander, to help. Use those three ideas at recess.

Theme: Listening closely because you may learn something new

Sometimes Grandma tells you the same story more than once. Listen patiently because she might tell you something new that you'll need to remember.

Discussion: Why is it important to listen to stories that older people tell?

Compare & Contrast: In the picture, you notice that the grandma is looking at an album and that reminds her of things that happened. Watch TV for one hour and see if you see the same commercial more than once. Compare that to Grandma telling the same story. What is the company on TV trying to get you to do? They want you to remember their product. Grandma may be doing the same thing. She wants you to remember her life stories.

Connection to Self: Plan a special time with your grandma, your grandpa, or an older person. It could be a tea party, lunch, building a bird house, playing ball in the yard, or a phone conversation. Ask him/her to tell you a story about when they were young. Write down or draw a picture of your special time. Bring it to school to share with the class during Character Chat.

Young-Thinker Activity (K-2): Play the "Telephone Game." Start the conversation by whispering one sentence with several details into one student's ear. The student then whispers into the next student's ear and so on until the entire class has participated. The last person should tell what he/she heard. Compare this to what the teacher said in the beginning.

In-depth Activity (3-5): Interview your grandma, your grandpa, or another older family member and write about their life. Were these happy memories? Compare their life to yours today. Which do you feel is better?

Practice on Your Own: Write a "thank you" note to or call your grandma or grandpa and tell them how much they mean to you.

Theme: Giving makes a difference

Donating your toys to kids who might not have any is a good way to show empathy toward others.

"Am I going to play with these anymore?"

KEEP   DONATE

Discussion: Why is it important to give to others? Lots of kids do not have toys of their own. If you have many toys, then sort through and donate some to a shelter or organization that collects toys for children. They will be happy and you will feel good about giving.

Compare & Contrast: What do the words "selfish" and "unselfish" mean? Look up both words and compare what these words mean in relationship to donating.

Connection to Self: Sometimes kids have two of the same toys or similar toys. Make a list of the duplicate toys you might have. You can include backpacks or pencils or crayons or gently used books. Look up on the community calendar for your town and/or call a community leader to get information on how to donate.

Young-Thinker Activity (K-2): *Service learning/Math concepts*. Join your class with an older-grade classroom and collect items for a donation. They can be pennies, gloves, books, and more. Your activity will be to count the items collected from your classroom and make a class thermometer chart that will count by 10s. Every time you reach ten, you can fill in the chart. This is a fun way to learn how to count by tens. When you reach the top, you will know how much you are helping someone else.

In-depth Activity (3-5): Research by clicking on the following link: http://www.feedingamerica.org/find-your-local-foodbank/. Write a paragraph about hunger in America, and find a food bank in your community that accepts donations or food. Many small towns have an organization called "Civic Concerns." They can direct you to people in need. Ask the principal if you could have an all-school drive and collect items to be donated. This is a service-learning project where everyone will benefit.

Practice on Your Own: About twice a year, practice going through all of your belongings and decide if you still use or need these items. Discuss with your parents/caregivers if they would be useful for others.

Theme: Listening to a friend shows you care

A good friend can tell when you're feeling sad.

She wants to listen and try to help you.

Discussion: Why is it important to be a good listener? Empathy comes in many forms. Being a good listener is one great way to show empathy. You don't have to fix the problem, just let the other person talk and be there for them.

Compare & Contrast: Using the **H5 T-Chart Skills Page** (pg. 131), on the left side write the body language of someone who doesn't listen and on the right side write the body language of a good listener. Then discuss with the class how a good friend acts when listening.

— ❀ ❀ ❀ ❀ ❀ ❀ ❀ ❀ ❀ ❀ ❀ ❀ ❀ ❀ —

Connection to Self: *Journal writing.* Finish this sentence: "When my friend has something important to tell me, I _____."

Young-Thinker Activity (K-2): Use the **H5 Hand Skills Page** (pg. 108) and have kids write on each finger and thumb important ways to be a good friend.

In-depth Activity (3-5): Make a list of the top ten words that describe a true friend. Have kids write a letter to their friend and tell why they like him/her so much. Make sure to include items from the list. Then have the kids write how they are going to be a good friend, too.

— ❀ ❀ ❀ ❀ ❀ ❀ ❀ ❀ ❀ ❀ ❀ ❀ ❀ ❀ —

Practice on Your Own: What have you learned from reading *Are You Empathetic Today?* Practice showing people you care by your words and actions.

Theme: Participating in a service-learning project

When we participate in a service project, we are aware and understanding of the needs in our community.

Discussion: Have you ever participated in a service-learning project in your community? What did you do? How do you think you served the community? Serving others is an honor, not a burden. When we give of ourselves, others benefit.

Compare & Contrast: Use the **H5 Donate vs. Trash Skills Page** (pg. 99) to put items in the correct category. Those that can be donated should be circled and those that can go into the trash can be crossed off. Can you come up with other items that can be donated?

Connection to Self: Watch the Salvation Army's #RedKettleReason video, https://www.youtube.com/watch?v=TKy-dIljLpg, and have kids write what they think it's about. Be sure to discuss that sometimes people can't donate time or goods, but they can donate money.

Young-Thinker Activity (K-2): Look at your lunch for the next three days. What parts do you throw away? Could you save them for a later snack? Ask your teacher if you could start a canned goods drive in your school.

In-depth Activity (3-5): *Journal writing.* Write what this means to you: "Serving others is an honor and not a burden." If you've participated in a service-learning project, be sure to include how you felt after you were finished. If you haven't participated in one, imagine what it would be like to be one of the characters in the illustration above.

Practice on Your Own: *Service learning.* Other than at Christmastime, get together with other kids and organize a way to give to others. Make a list of five different opportunities. Some examples are a coat drive, a toy drive, collecting bottles and cans to donate the money, donating backpacks for school, collecting pennies to donate, collecting diapers for infants and pet food for needy pets in shelters.

Theme: Being a good sport

Discussion: Why do players line up and say "good game" to each other? How can being a good sport extend to games we play in school? Should you say "good game" when a game is finished? Sportsmanship is very important in games. It is important to show respect for the players and the rules.

Compare & Contrast: Whether you win a game or lose, you need to display appropriate team behavior. Go to this link and read what coaches say about the importance of the handshake: http://journalstar.com/sports/columnists/rj-hambleton/handshake-ritual-remains-a-big-part-of-sports/article_ba76fba2-c87d-52d8-9889-07e5485f7121.html. What are the pros and cons of having a handshake at the end of a game?

Connection to Self: *Journal writing.* Whether you play a sport or not, describe how you would end a game. Would you include a handshake or positive words such as "good game," "nice job," or some other positive phrase, or would you do something different?

Young-Thinker Activity (K-2): Make two lines in your class that symbolize two teams and then have the two groups give handshakes and say the words "You are great!"

In-depth Activity (3-5): Do research on when the first handshake began in sports and what sport started the ritual. Write a paragraph about why the handshake is so important in sports.

Practice on Your Own: Give a handshake after any game you play. Even if you play a card game or checkers, give a handshake when you are done, win or lose! Be the one who initiates the handshake and you will be surprised that others will, too.

Theme: Be aware of how others are feeling and show kindness

Discussion: Why is it important to be aware of how others are feeling and to show kindness? Doing something nice comes from your heart. Remember, it is not about what YOU feel, but more about how others will feel.

Compare & Contrast: Focus on the first image and the mom sitting in the chair. Why is she slouching? Why are her shoes off? Why is she touching her head? Now focus on the boy. How is his face different than his mom's? What is the energy level of the boy? How does the energy level of the boy differ from that of the mom?

Connection to Self: *Journal writing.* Describe a time when you were totally exhausted. Did anyone bring you food or help you? Be sure to include lots of details.

Young-Thinker Activity (K-2): If someone is sick or in the hospital, have students make one large "get well" card to send from the class or everyone can make their own card.

In-depth Activity (3-5): *Persuasive writing.* Write a persuasive paragraph as to why it's important to bring happiness and kindness to people who are sick, either at a hospital or at home.

Practice on Your Own: Be aware of family members who are tired and exhausted. How can you help them?

Honest

How can I teach honesty today?

Being honest to avoid lying, cheating, and stealing is doing the right thing. We need to go back to the concepts of right and wrong. As teachers, it is your job, as a healthy role model, to reinforce these honest concepts. Kids need us to guide them and to instill these core values. Consider teaching these skills as an honor and a privilege. Consider every opportunity to be a learning experience for them.

Being a fair and consistent role model and someone who cares about the students will be the best that the students can get. If you are the enforcer and punisher, kids will only develop a negative view of teachers. Show students how to make positive decisions each and every day with love and compassion.

Words and phrases that you can use in your classroom:
- "Is that the best choice for you?"
- "Who is responsible for you?"
- "Remember: think before you act."
- "Do the right thing!"
- "I am proud of you for being honest."
- "Honesty is the best policy."

Encourage healthy body language:
- Stand up straight
- Put your shoulders back
- If someone makes a mistake, don't stare
- Have a forgiving heart

THURSDAY is all about being HONEST!

Theme: Bring on the honesty!

Read this book before you begin.

Find the definition of the character trait (honest).
Have the kids name five ways to be honest as shown in the book. Post answers for all to see.

Try This!
Have all kids repeat the mantra on this page five times out loud: **"I will be truthful and fair to others."**

Character question: How do they feel after repeating the mantra? This mantra is to help kids feel empowered to do their best. Teachers can encourage kids that each should be doing their best all day.

End of Day Character Challenge: What was the mantra they said in the morning? "I will be truthful and fair to others." Give high-fives to all students.

Try this! Each day when you wake up, say out loud,

"I will be truthful and fair to others."

Theme: Answering parents truthfully

Discussion: What does "sincerely" mean? When we speak sincerely, are we speaking from our heart or just answering the question? How do people know when we are speaking sincerely?

Compare & Contrast: Make a list of words and/or actions that show sincerity. The Macmillan Dictionary online version defines sincerity as: *an honest way of behaving that shows that you really mean what you say or do.* Next, create a list of words and/or actions that don't show sincerity. Discuss the concept of doing the right thing.

——— ⚬❦⚬ ⚬ ❦⚬ ⚬ ❦⚬ ⚬ ❦⚬ ⚬ ❦⚬ ⚬ ❦⚬ ——–

Connection to Self: *Partner interview.* What chores are you responsible for at home? Do you like them? Is there a chore you'd like to do instead? Name the chore. What happens if you don't give your best effort when doing your chores?

Young-Thinker Activity (K-2): Draw a picture of how your bedroom would look after you cleaned it. Take it home and hang it on your bedroom door as a reminder.

In-depth Activity (3-5): *Journal writing.* It's tempting to not tell the truth at times because we are afraid we will get in trouble. Write about a time when you were tempted to lie but instead told the truth. How did it feel to be honest?

——— ⚬❦⚬ ⚬ ❦⚬ ⚬ ❦⚬ ⚬ ❦⚬ ⚬ ❦⚬ ⚬ ❦⚬ ——–

Practice on Your Own: Have kids practice this chant: "Honesty, honesty, the way to always be!"

Theme: Asking for help

While walking to school with Papa, you tell him you have a spelling test. When he asks if you studied, you're honest and say you're not quite ready.

"Papa, can you help me with my words?"

Discussion: When should we ask for help? Is it only when we don't understand something? Can it be to practice, such as spelling words or math problems? Whom can you ask for help? It's important to be honest with ourselves when we need help.

Compare & Contrast: *Journal writing.* Describe a time when you were prepared for a test and a time when you weren't prepared for a test. Which situation would you rather be in?

———————————————————

Connection to Self: Have students fill out the **H5 Becoming a Better Me! Asking for Help Skills Page** (pg. 92) to track those areas where they need help for a week. Did the chart help? Use the chart as often as necessary.

Young-Thinker Activity (K-2): Using the **H5 Hand Skills Page** (pg. 108), have students write or draw images of activities they would ask for help with and who would help them.

In-depth Activity (3-5): *Role play.* Pair students and have them act out one of these situations: asking for help from the librarian to get a book, asking for help to peel a banana, asking for help to tie shoes. Swap roles to make sure that each student gets to be the helper and the one being helped. Brainstorm other situations to role play asking for help.

———————————————————

Practice on Your Own: Encourage kids to fill out the **H5 High 5ver!** (pg. 109) form when they were honest about not being prepared and how they will change their behavior.

Theme: Thinking about the feelings of a friend

Discussion: What would you do if a friend got a new haircut and you didn't like it? What would you say? What if you got a new haircut and a friend told you it looked terrible? How would you feel?

Compare & Contrast: Compare this image with the first image of "Think before you speak and act" on page 50. How are they similar and how are they different?

—⋅෴ ℓ⋅ ⦚ ⦂෴ ⋅ℴ ℅⋅ ⦂ℴ ⦂෴ ℅⋅ ⦚⋅ ⋅෴ ℓ ⋅෴⦂ ⦚ ⋅ℴ ℅෴ ⋅—

Connection to Self: *Journal writing.* Have you ever had someone tell you that they didn't like your hair/shirt/toy? How did you react? Write a short paragraph describing the situation.

Young-Thinker Activity (K-2): *Role play.* Have three pairs of students role play the following situations: one has a new haircut, one has a new shirt, and one has a new pair of shoes. Instruct the kids to be completely honest the first time. Then, have the kids use kinder words as shown in the illustration. Decide as a group which way is better.

In-depth Activity (3-5): *Role play.* Have a pair of students role play the situation in the image. The first time, the student should be brutally honest about the new haircut. Now, role play again, but have the student use a filter as shown in the illustration. Discuss ways that kids can use a filter to not hurt someone's feelings.

—⋅෴ ℓ⋅ ⦚ ⦂෴ ⋅ℴ ℅⋅ ⦂ℴ ⦂෴ ℅⋅ ⦚⋅ ⋅෴ ℓ ⋅෴⦂ ⦚ ⋅ℴ ℅෴ ⋅—

Practice on Your Own: Sometimes our feelings get hurt by things that people say when they are being "honest." Use kind words when questioned in situations like the one shown in this image.

Theme: Think before you make a mistake like cheating

Discussion: Is it ever a good idea to cheat? When you cheat, who gets hurt? Is it just you or does the person whose ideas you are stealing get hurt as well? Why shouldn't we cheat? What can you do so you don't feel like you should cheat?

Compare & Contrast: Use the **H5 Venn Diagram Skills Page** (pg. 134) to chart the differences and similarities between the two above images. How could the second image have been different? What if the second boy let the first boy cheat?

Connection to Self: *Journal writing.* When you make a mistake, how do you feel? What would you do differently next time?

Young-Thinker Activity (K-2): Have students complete the **H5 I Am Honest Word Search Skills Page** (pg. 120). Afterward, cross off the words that are the opposite of what it means to be honest.

In-depth Activity (3-5): *Role play.* Have students pair up and act out the two images. Afterward, have a class discussion: What do you think the boy on the right is thinking about what the other boy is doing? In the second picture, how does the boy on the left change? What do you think made him change his mind about cheating?

Practice on Your Own: Have students practice this chant: "I will think before I cheat; that's a fact I will repeat."

Theme: What happens when you lie?

Discussion: What may happen if you lie a lot? How do you hurt yourself when you are dishonest? Do you think it was wrong for the girl in the middle to say that she used to be friends with the other girl? Do friends lie to each other?

Compare & Contrast: How does the girl look in the second image compared to the first image? Why is there such a difference? How could she avoid feeling the way she does in the second image? Discuss the similarities and differences between both images.

———————————————

Connection to Self: *Journal writing.* Has a friend ever lied to you? How did you feel? Did you forgive that person?

Young-Thinker Activity (K-2): *Discussion.* Sometimes we forget to be honest and our friends find out. Do you think the girl in the striped shirt would be friends with the girl next to the lockers? Why or why not?

In-depth Activity (3-5): Have the students complete the **H5 H-O-N-E-S-T Acrostic Skills Page** (pg. 110). If they need help, have each complete the **H5 H-O-N-E-S-T Acrostic Word List Skills Page** (pg. 111) first. Take a poll: Which words did most students use? Which words would the students use to describe themselves? List the words and the rank highest to lowest. Which word was the winner? Which word had the fewest uses?

———————————————

Practice on Your Own: Why did Benjamin Franklin say, "Honesty is the best policy"?

Theme: Paying for things

Discussion: Is it right to steal? What should the boy wearing the glasses do instead of stealing the cookie? Is the boy with the tray a good friend? How do you know?

Compare & Contrast: Make a list of what's happening in each image. What are the similarities and the differences?

——·⸙ᴄ.·ꙮ ꙮ.·⸱᛬·ꙮ.·ꙮ᛬ꙮ.·ꙮ.·⸱᛬.ᴄ.·ꙮ᛬ꙮ.·ꙮ᛬·——

Connection to Self: *Journal writing.* Finish this sentence, "If I found a wallet on the sidewalk, I would _____."

Young-Thinker Activity (K-2): Have students decorate the **H5 Cookie! Skills Page** (pg. 98) and fill in the name of the person with whom they would share their cookie. Discuss if you should take things that don't belong to you. What are the consequences of taking something that doesn't belong to you?

In-depth Activity (3-5): *Journal writing.* Write a persuasive paragraph about why stealing is wrong.

——·⸙ᴄ.·ꙮ ꙮ.·⸱᛬·ꙮ.·ꙮ᛬ꙮ.·ꙮ.·⸱᛬.ᴄ.·ꙮ᛬ꙮ.·ꙮ᛬·——

Practice on Your Own: Notice if someone brings only one thing to eat at lunch. If possible, share your snacks.

Theme: Being honest when working on a service-learning project

Discussion: Why is it important to help others in our community? Watch www.cbsnews.com/videos/8-year-old-boy-creates-charitable-lemonade-stand and discuss the impact that this young boy had on his community.

Compare & Contrast: What would happen if you collected money for a service project but then didn't turn the money in to the organization? Make a list of those who are affected by turning in the money and those who are affected when the money isn't turned in.

———————————————————————————

Connection to Self: *Journal writing.* After watching the video in the **Discussion** and seeing that Logan wants to be a super helpful guy, how can you be a super helpful person?

Young-Thinker Activity (K-2): *Math concepts.* Have kids practice making change by using the **H5 Let's Make Change! Skills Page** (pg. 127).

In-depth Activity (3-5): *Service learning.* Organize a canned food drive for a local community. Have kids bring in cans and then have a representative from the organization visit the classroom to pick up the donations and to speak about how their organization helps the community.

———————————————————————————

Practice on Your Own: Encourage students to understand Anne Frank's comment: "No one has ever become poor by giving."

Theme: Making the right choice

When your younger brother spills his juice on the couch cushion, you help him clean it up even though he wants to hide it.

"No, no, we have to take care of this."

"Oh, okay."

Discussion: Is it hard to make the right choice? Why does it seem easier to cover up a mistake? But, is it the right thing to do to cover up our mistakes? What important ideas in the text will help you feel more honest in your daily situations?

Compare & Contrast: Use the **H5 Venn Diagram Skills Page** (pg. 134) to detail out what would happen if the mess in the image was cleaned up and if it wasn't cleaned up. Be sure to include all that you see in the image. Use your imagination about the mess not being cleaned up.

—⋆∘੦੦·∘·੦·੦··੦੦·∘∘·∘·੦·∘∘੦·∘·੦੦—

Connection to Self: *Journal writing.* Have you ever made a mess and tried to hide it? Write at least one paragraph about what happened, making sure to include a lot of details. Don't forget to include the end result.

Young-Thinker Activity (K-2): Use the **H5 3-Box Sequence Strip Skills Page** (pg. 90) to detail the following: making a mess, trying to hide the mess, and cleaning up the mess that was made. Add words to give clues to the drawings.

In-depth Activity (3-5): *Role play.* Group students and have them role play the above scene. Change it up a bit and have the sister not find the mess OR have a parent walk in at this exact moment OR have the boy going to the sister for help. How did the outcome change in each situation, if at all?

—⋆∘੦੦·∘·੦·੦··੦੦·∘∘·∘·੦·∘∘੦·∘·੦੦—

Practice on Your Own: Realize mistakes happen and that we need to stay calm. Teach them the 4:6:8 calm breathing rule: Breathe in for four counts, hold for six counts, and breathe out through the mouth for eight counts. Repeat once more.

Theme: Being a reliable person

Honest people are trustworthy,
and others know that they can rely on you.

Discussion: What does "trustworthy" mean? The Macmillan Dictionary online version defines it as: *able to be trusted as honest, safe, or reliable.* Can kids be trustworthy or can only adults be trustworthy? Why or why not?

Compare & Contrast: What does it take to be a good babysitter? What about a bad babysitter? Use the **H5 Double Hand Skills Page** (pg. 102) to list five details of a good babysitter on the right hand and five details of a bad babysitter on the left hand. Which one would you want to have watch you?

Connection to Self: *Journal writing.* What does it mean to be reliable? The Macmillan Dictionary online version defines it as: *a reliable person is someone who you can trust to behave well, work hard, or do what you expect them to do.* Has anyone called you reliable? Write a short paragraph about when you were reliable, whether someone called you that or not.

Young-Thinker Activity (K-2): Teach kids this chant: "I can rely on you. You can rely on me. That's what friends are for." For hand movements, have kids point to themselves at "I" and point to others for "you," and then hands in the air for "That's what friends are for."

In-depth Activity (3-5): *Partner interview.* Have students interview for a babysitting job. Have the interviewer ask questions such as "Tell me how I know you're honest" "How will you keep my child safe?" and "Tell me about how you're a hard worker." Have the students switch roles. Afterward, discuss as a group: Was it hard to come up with the answers? Which question was the hardest to answer?

Practice on Your Own: Notice when others are working hard. Fill out a **H5 High 5ver** (pg. 109) form and turn it in to the teacher.

Theme: Taking something that you want

Sometimes you may think it's a good idea to take something you want.

"Stop!
Give that toy back."

Discussion: Have you ever wanted to take something that wasn't yours? What did you do to stop yourself? How do you think the person who owned the item would have felt if you had really taken it?

Compare & Contrast: Compare this image with the image of "Being careful with others' belongings" on page 29. What are the differences and similarities?

Connection to Self: *Partner interview.* Each student should have the opportunity to answer these questions: What would you do if a friend took your toy? Would you still be friends?

Young-Thinker Activity (K-2): Have students draw and color their favorite stuffed animal or toy. Discuss how each would feel if someone took it.

In-depth Activity (3-5): *Creative writing.* Write a detailed story about someone who takes something that doesn't belong to him/her but returns the item in the end. Show how the character changes from the beginning to the end. Be sure to have at least two characters: one main character and one secondary character.

Practice on Your Own: How could you get a toy you wanted without taking it?

Theme: Returning something that doesn't belong to you and admitting your mistake

It might be scary, but you'll know in your heart that you did the right thing by returning the toy.

"Here, this belongs to you."

Discussion: Is it hard to tell the truth sometimes? How can we make sure that it isn't hard? (Practice apologizing and telling the truth. Also, don't lie, cheat, or steal.)

Compare & Contrast: Make a list of the differences and similarities between the boy in the striped shirt and the boy with the car. Be sure to include words each may say and actions each may do.

———⁘⁙⁘⁙⁘⁙⁘⁙⁘⁙⁘⁙⁘⁙⁘⁙⁘⁙⁘⁙⁘⁙———

Connection to Self: *Journal writing.* Pretend you've taken something that doesn't belong to you. Write a script of what you would say to the owner of what you've taken. Be sure to include what you did, your apology, and how you are going to change.

Young-Thinker Activity (K-2): Pair students and have the pairs discuss and/or role play the following: How can the boy in the striped shirt tell that the other boy is sorry for trying to take the toy (i.e., face, posture, words he is using, etc.)?

In-depth Activity (3-5): *Role play.* Have three kids role play the image above. Rotate students so that each is able to take the role of the older sibling, the friend, and the younger brother. How did each feel when they played their role?

———⁘⁙⁘⁙⁘⁙⁘⁙⁘⁙⁘⁙⁘⁙⁘⁙⁘⁙⁘⁙⁘⁙———

Practice on Your Own: Realize that you will make mistakes, but it's our responsibility to make a different choice.

Theme: Following the rules

When playing a sport, everyone needs to follow the rules.

Discussion: Why is it important to follow rules in a game? When playing a sport, is it better to follow the rules or to play how you want to play? Why?

Compare & Contrast: Select a sport and make a list of how the game would be played if played by the rules and another list if players didn't play by the rules. Are there any similarities?

———

Connection to Self: *Journal writing.* Write a detailed entry about a time when you played fairly or when someone else didn't play fairly. Be sure to include a beginning, middle, and end, as well as the outcome.

Young-Thinker Activity (K-2): *Discussion.* What would happen if there were no rules in school?

In-depth Activity (3-5): Have kids research the basic rules of a sport they choose (e.g., number of players on the team, number of players during play/on the field, is there a referee [if yes, how many?], etc.). Come together as a group and discuss the similarities and differences between the sports chosen.

———

Practice on Your Own: Playing fairly doesn't just happen in a sport; it happens on the playground, in the classroom, lots of different places. Encourage fair play by having the kids fill out an **H5 High 5ver!** (pg. 109) form and turn it in to the teacher.

Theme: Playing fair

Playing fairly allows each person to have fun and practice being a good sport.

Discussion: What does it mean to be a "good sport"? Are you a good sport only when your team wins? Are you a good sport when your team loses?

Compare & Contrast: Make a list of words and/or actions that details how the winning team demonstrates good sportsmanship. Make another list of words and/or actions that shows how a losing team demonstrated good sportsmanship.

—⁓⁓⁓⁓⁓⁓⁓⁓⁓⁓—

Connection to Self: *Journal writing.* Write about a time when you played fairly. Be sure to give lots of details and include a beginning, middle, and end.

Young-Thinker Activity (K-2): Teach the kids the following chant: "I will play fairly, all day, every day. I'm a good sport, all day long." Repeat two times.

In-depth Activity (3-5): *Poster.* Partner students and have each pair create a "play fair" or "be a good sport" poster for their chosen sport. Have kids include words that describe being a good sport or playing fair. Hang up the poster and discuss the attributes of each.

—⁓⁓⁓⁓⁓⁓⁓⁓⁓⁓—

Practice on Your Own: Have kids practice "I will play fair on the field and in class."

Theme: How would you feel if you stole something but didn't get caught?

Discussion: If you decided to take something that didn't belong to you and no one saw you, how do you think you would feel? What should you do before you take something that doesn't belong to you? (Stop and think.)

Compare & Contrast: Compare this image with the first image in "Paying for things" on page 64. What are the similarities and differences? Do you think the boy in this image would still take more than one candy if he had a friend with him? What might the friend say?

Connection to Self: *Journal writing.* Put yourself in the shoes of the boy. Why are you taking all of the candy? It looks like you're not going to get caught. How do you feel? If you think about it, though, how do you really feel? Do you think you'd do this again?

Young-Thinker Activity (K-2): *Discussion.* Looking at the illustration, would an honest person do this? What does the little sign say? Why do you think the boy is taking all of the candy?

In-depth Activity (3-5): *Scene writing.* Write a detailed script of the above illustration and then the scene that follows. Perhaps a friend saw the boy take all of the candy OR perhaps the boy begins to eat the candy and a parent questions where the candy came from. How does the boy respond in these new scenes? How does he feel? Does he lie to cover up his stealing?

Practice on Your Own: Teach kids this chant: "I will stop and think before I act." Have them clap "I will," then raise their palm for "stop," then point to their head for "think" and do a thumbs-up with both hands for "before I act." Repeat several times a day or week.

Grateful

How can I teach gratefulness today?

Gratefulness comes from the heart. Again, this is the muscle that needs to be nurtured in many people. This is our favorite book of the series because it is the most needed today. People seem to be grateful for things and stuff. We need to teach them to go back to the basics and learn to be grateful for their loved ones, a bed to sleep in, and food to eat. In the United States, we have opportunities to have so many things that other countries do not have. As Americans, we need to appreciate what we have and then give and share with others who are far less fortunate. Human beings can learn to care, reach out to others, and help.

Words and phrases that you can use in your classroom:
- "Look for what you are good at and practice to get better."
- "Don't be selfish."
- "Help others."
- "Work together for the greater good."
- "You can do it!"
- "There you go."
- "I am proud of you."
- "Thank you for being ready."

Encourage healthy body language:
- Smile
- Give high-fives
- Cheer for others
- Stand up straight
- Try your best

FRIDAY is all about being GRATEFUL!

Theme: Bring on the gratefulness!

Read this book before you begin.

Find the definition of the character trait (grateful).
Have the kids name five ways to be grateful as shown in the book. Post answers for all to see.

Try This!
Have all kids repeat the mantra on this page five times out loud: **"I am grateful for my home, family, friends, happiness, and my health."**

Character question: How do they feel after repeating the mantra? This mantra is to help kids feel empowered to do their best. Teachers can encourage kids that each should be doing their best all day.

End of Day Character Challenge: What was the mantra they said in the morning? "I am grateful for my home, family, friends, happiness, and my health." Give high-fives to all students.

Try this!
Each day when you wake up, say out loud,
"I am grateful for my home, family, friends, happiness, and my health."

"Mom and Dad,
I just want to tell you that I love you."

Theme: What are you grateful for?

Look around and notice that you have a bed to sleep in,
food to eat, and clothes to wear.
Remind yourself that you are grateful for many things.

Discussion: Gratefulness comes from your heart. Why is it important to be grateful? What is the purpose of having a grateful journal?

Compare & Contrast: Compare what people had in the year 1900 and the current year. Did they have televisions, cars, electricity, movies, computers, video games, etc.? What did they have? Do you think they were grateful for what they had?

Connection to Self: Use the **H5 I'm Grateful for… Skills Page** (pg. 117) and list those things that you are grateful for in your life. This list can include people, things, places, etc. Be sure to date your list. Review the list in thirty days. Has anything changed? Would you change your list by adding or subtracting?

Young-Thinker Activity (K-2): Draw a picture of something that you are grateful for. It can be a picture of someone or something in your life.

In-depth Activity (3-5): The Macmillan Dictionary online version defines grateful as: *feeling that you want to thank someone because they have given you something or have done something for you.* Create a "thank you" card for or write a letter to someone you are grateful for. Remember to include why you are grateful for them in your card/letter.

Practice on Your Own: Sometimes we forget to be grateful. Hang your list from the **Connection to Self** activity someplace where you'll see it every day.

Theme: How can you show gratefulness to your family and others?

Thank your family and caregivers for their love.
Hugs and kisses show you love them, too.

Discussion: What words and/or actions can you use that will show your family and others that you care about them? How do others feel when we show our gratitude toward them? How do you feel? How often should we tell people we are grateful for them?

Compare & Contrast: Use the **H5 T-Chart Skills Page** (pg. 131) to compare and contrast "Grateful" and "Selfish." Make a list of words that describe each concept. Discuss how others respond to you when you are grateful and when you are selfish.

Connection to Self: Using the **H5 Hand Skills Page** (pg. 108), show five ways that others express gratefulness to you.

Young-Thinker Activity (K-2): Draw a picture of someone you love. Write their name on your picture. Give your picture to that person and tell them why you love them.

In-depth Activity (3-5): Do the **H5 Gratefulness Challenge Skills Page** (pg. 107). For five days, keep track of people who make you feel grateful or of times when you feel grateful. Share the results with the class, with a small group, or with a partner.

Practice on Your Own: When we have a bad day, we may feel sad. Review your **H5 Gratefulness Challenge Skills Page** to remind yourself how you felt at those times when you were feeling most grateful.

Theme: Showing gratefulness to animals

Feed and play with your pet. You'll know they are grateful when they wag their tails and cuddle in your lap.

"Here we go, Oreo!"

Discussion: Do you have an animal that you take care of? How do you give it attention and show it love? Do animals show gratitude to humans? Watch this short video and discuss. https://www.youtube.com/watch?v=H3wrPd-f8LU.

Compare & Contrast: Compare this illustration to the cover of *Are You Empathetic Today?* What are the similarities and differences?

Connection to Self: *Service learning.* Plan a class fundraiser for a local animal shelter. Decide on the shelter by a vote and then choose items to donate. You could donate food, toys, treats, or other items that the animal shelter needs. Afterward, write a journal entry describing what it felt like to donate to the shelter.

Young-Thinker Activity (K-2): Choose an animal to adopt. Draw a picture of the animal and why you want to adopt it.

In-depth Activity (3-5): *Realistic fiction writing.* Watch this video about helping a dolphin: https://www.youtube.com/watch?v=2gvgkHSyKFE. Where does the rescue take place? What was the problem? How does the dolphin react? Imagine that you are the diver. Write a realistic fiction piece of your experiences helping this dolphin. Be sure to include how you felt.

Practice on Your Own: If you have a pet at home, make it a habit to give lots of love and cuddles. If you don't have a pet, ask your parents/caregiver if you can visit an animal shelter.

Theme: How will school help you succeed?

Hey! You're smart and can learn new things, like reading, math, and how to write stories.
Knowledge will help you make good decisions your whole life.
Be grateful for every time you learn something new.

7x7=   7x7=49
7x8=   x8=56
7x9=   7x9=

Thank your teachers for how hard they work to help you learn.

Discussion: Why is it important to learn new things? Can we be successful in life and in the community if we aren't learning? Should we only learn things that are easy? Why is it important to be challenged in schoolwork?

Compare & Contrast: What is your favorite subject? What is your least favorite subject? Is one subject more challenging? Is one easier?

— ⋆⋅∘⋆⋆∘⋆⋆∘⋆∘⋆∘⋆⋆∘⋆⋆∘⋆∘⋆⋆∘⋆∘⋆∘⋆ —

Connection to Self: *Journal writing.* What would the world be like if we didn't have to go to school? How would you learn things? Who would teach you? Do you think this would work?

Young-Thinker Activity (K-2): Read the last page of the story of *Are You Grateful Today?* (the kids reading books) and teach the students the mantra, "I will practice, practice and never give up."

In-depth Activity (3-5): *Debate.* Which subjects should be taught on the moon? A space station is starting a school on the moon and is looking for two subjects to teach. Pair or group students. Have them pick one subject (math, music, reading, science, social studies) and list the pros and cons as to why their subject should be taught on the moon.

— ⋆⋅∘⋆⋆∘⋆⋆∘⋆∘⋆∘⋆⋆∘⋆⋆∘⋆∘⋆⋆∘⋆∘⋆∘⋆ —

Practice on Your Own: Homework is the ultimate practice for learning. Keep track of your completed homework in a notebook for a week.

Theme: Discover your talents!

Discussion: Oftentimes we compare ourselves to others and forget our talents. How do we feel when we compare ourselves to others? Are we showing gratefulness toward ourselves when we think others are better than we are? If we want to get better at something, what do we need to do? (Practice)

Compare & Contrast: Compare the second page above to "Let's try something new" images on page 16. How do you think the boy is feeling on page 16? Do you think he's grateful that he's decided to learn to play the trombone? Let's assume the boy above feels very confident about playing the tuba. Do you think he's grateful for his musical ability?

— ⋅∾꙰ ꙫ ⋅◌ ꙴ⋅◌ ⋅∙ ꙶꙷ⋅∙◌ ⋅◌꙳◌ ꙫ⋅ ◌⋅∾꙰ ꙫ ⋅◌꙳◌ ◌ ⋅◌ ꙶꙷ⋅—

Connection to Self: *Journal writing.* What do you do that makes you the happiest? Do you think this is a talent? Why or why not?

Young-Thinker Activity (K-2): Draw a picture of your talent. Some examples could be playing baseball, swimming, writing a story, creating a picture, playing a trumpet, baking cookies, or flying a kite.

In-depth Activity (3-5): *Talent show.* Encourage all kids to participate. Kids would have two minutes to showcase their talent. Break up the talent show over several days so as not to disrupt class time. If kids don't want to showcase their talent, have them write a short essay describing their talent.

— ⋅∾꙰ ꙫ ⋅◌ ꙴ⋅◌ ⋅∙ ꙶꙷ⋅∙◌ ⋅◌꙳◌ ꙫ⋅ ◌⋅∾꙰ ꙫ ⋅◌꙳◌ ◌ ⋅◌ ꙶꙷ⋅—

Practice on Your Own: To remind yourself that you have talents, be sure to say this to yourself often, "I'm grateful for being able to _____" (fill in the blank).

Theme: What words do you use to show gratefulness toward yourself?

Discussion: What words do you use to describe yourself? Are they positive or negative words? Why would anyone use negative words to describe themselves? Does this show gratitude for ourselves when we speak negatively?

Compare & Contrast: Using the above discussion, make a list of words the kids said. Categorize the words by: appearance, talent, outlook/personality, skills, etc. Which category has the most words? Which has the least? Can you make a comparison between the two lists?

Connection to Self: *Journal writing.* Watch the "Dove Real Beauty Sketches" video: https://www.youtube.com/watch?v=XpaOjMXyJGk. If you were one of the people in this video, how do you think you'd react to seeing how someone else described you?

Young-Thinker Activity (K-2): *Discussion.* Bring in a picture or draw a picture of yourself all dressed up for a special occasion. What are you wearing? How is your hair styled? What does your face look like? People often say that when we look our best, we feel our best. How do you describe yourself in the picture?

In-depth Activity (3-5): Write each student's name on a slip of paper and have students pick one from a basket. Alone, have the students write positive qualities about the person whose name appears on the slip of paper. Then, pair students up with the person whose name appears on the paper and have each read to the other what is written. Give the paper to the person whose name is on it. Keep in your Character Folder as a reminder of the positive thoughts that person had about you.

Practice on Your Own: Each day this week while you are brushing your teeth in the morning, say to yourself, "I'm fantastic! I love my hair! I love my face! I love myself!"

Theme: What words and actions do you use to show gratefulness toward others?

Remember, what matters most are your positive thoughts, words, and actions, not what you wear or things you have.

"Thank you for this meal!"

Discussion: What do you say or how do you act to show others you are grateful for them? How do you think others feel when you say these things or do these things? Why is it important to express our gratefulness to others?

Compare & Contrast: *Situation.* A group of kids just lost a game of kickball at recess. Compare and contrast how a grateful person and an ungrateful person would act.

Connection to Self: *Journal writing.* Finish this sentence: "I show gratefulness to my family and friends when_____."

Young-Thinker Activity (K-2): Have kids complete the **H5 I Am Grateful for YOU! Word Search Skills Page** (pg. 118). Review any words that are new to the students.

In-depth Activity (3-5): Have students complete the **H5 G-R-A-T-E-F-U-L Acrostic Skills Page** (pg. 105). Use the **H5 G-R-A-T-E-F-U-L Acrostic Word List Skills Page** (pg. 106) for help. Discuss the words for each letter.

Practice on Your Own: Find one person each day for five days and tell them why you are grateful for them.

Theme: What do you do when you want something?

Discussion: How do you get the things you want? Do parents have an endless stream of money? Parents have to earn their money through their jobs. Do you have chores that allow you to earn money to buy the things you want? If you don't, ask your parents if you can do chores to earn money.

Compare & Contrast: What does a grateful person look like on his/her birthday? What does an ungrateful person look like on his/her birthday?

———— ❦ ———

Connection to Self: *Journal writing.* Write about a time when you really wanted something. Did you get it? How? What did you have to do? Did you get it right away or did you have to wait? How did it feel once you finally got what you wanted?

Young-Thinker Activity (K-2): Draw a picture of you doing a chore so that you can earn some money to buy your favorite item. How many times would you have to do that chore to earn enough money to buy it?

In-depth Activity (3-5): *Math concepts.* Research the price of something that you really want, such as a game, a bike, a phone, etc. Now determine how many hours of chores you would have to complete in order to buy the item. Use $2.00 an hour as your pay. How many hours do you need to work to have enough money?

———— ❦ ———

Practice on Your Own: Write a "thank you" note to your parents telling them how grateful you are to them for the work they do in order to give you a home, food, clothing, and extras.

Theme: We are grateful when friends support us

Discussion: What words do you use to encourage your friends? How does encouragement show that you care for your friends? Do you ever think that when you share your belongings your friend is grateful?

Compare & Contrast: Imagine that you're at the park with your friend and you are both rock climbing. You've never rock climbed before. Your friend is an expert. How would you feel if your friend ignored you as you struggled to climb? How would you feel if your friend said encouraging words to you?

—⁕⁘⁙⁘⁕⁙⁘⁕⁙⁘⁕⁙⁘⁕⁙⁘—

Connection to Self: *Journal writing.* Write about a time when a friend encouraged you. What happened? What did he/she say? How did you feel?

Young-Thinker Activity (K-2): *Partner project.* What is your favorite activity to do with your friends? Spend two minutes and tell a partner about something you do with your friends. Then, your partner will spend two minutes telling you what he/she likes to do with his/her friends.

In-depth Activity (3-5): *Persuasive writing.* Write a persuasive paragraph using one of the two images above to show why it's important to support a friend.

—⁕⁘⁙⁘⁕⁙⁘⁕⁙⁘⁕⁙⁘⁕⁙⁘—

Practice on Your Own: Remind yourself to always be a positive person toward your friends by saying, "I'll help others as best as I can."

Theme: Being a good role model

When you act as a good role model for others, they will be thankful for your leadership.

Discussion: What makes a person a good role model? Looking at the illustration, how are these kids being good role models? What are they doing? Is one clearly the leader? How can you tell?

Compare & Contrast: Compare the image "What it takes to be a good leader" on page 22 to this image. Who is the leader in each image? How can you tell?

Connection to Self: Fill out **H5 I Am _____ Web Diagram Skills Page** (pg. 113). Have kids write "A Good Role Model" on the blank line in the Skills Page Title. In the center circle, write the name of the person you think is a good role model. On the spokes, write why that person is a good role model.

Young-Thinker Activity (K-2): Write a "thank you" letter to or make a "thank you" card for someone who has been a good role model to you. Be sure to say why he/she is such a good role model and then give it to that person.

In-depth Activity (3-5): *Service learning.* Have the class choose a local charity to help. Have them make posters to advertise what they are collecting (e.g., canned goods, pennies, gently used clothes, etc.) and post throughout the school. Perhaps have the students talk about the fundraiser on the morning announcements. Help the students be good role models for the collection by encouraging each to participate and to visit each class in their grade (or entire school if allowed) to encourage others to participate. When the fundraiser is over, have someone from the charity come into the classroom and discuss how the class is going to make an impact on the charity.

Practice on Your Own: To remind yourself to always be a good role model, say this often: "My actions and words mean something to others. Remember to say and do good deeds so I can be a role model to others."

Theme: Having pride of ownership

Your mom or dad will be grateful if you are helpful around the house.
Clean up your room.
Set the table.
Do your chores without being asked.

We feel happy when we work together to accomplish our goals.

Discussion: What is pride of ownership? (To feel proud of something that belongs to you.) How do we treat our belongings? When we are proud of our things, we take extra-special care.

Compare & Contrast: What does a grateful person look like who has pride of ownership? What does an ungrateful person look like who doesn't have pride of ownership? Make a list of words for both types of people and discuss how being grateful has a direct relationship to pride of ownership.

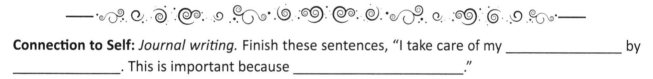

Connection to Self: *Journal writing.* Finish these sentences, "I take care of my _____ by _____. This is important because _____."

Young-Thinker Activity (K-2): *Discussion.* What part of your home do you have pride of ownership (e.g., bedroom, toy room, etc.)? How do you show your pride of ownership (e.g., clean up, organize, etc.)?

In-depth Activity (3-5): *Math concepts.* Is it easier to clean a whole house on your own or with others? Imagine it takes 20 minutes to clean one room in a six-room home. How long would it take you to clean the whole house on your own? How long would it take if two people were cleaning and they worked at the same pace (20 minutes x 6= 120 minutes for one person; 120 minutes ÷ 2 = 60 minutes)? How long if 3 people worked at the same pace? Figure out how long it would take if 4, 5, and 6 people helped out. Do you have pride of ownership in the rooms you've cleaned? What does cleaning rooms in your home and taking good care of your home have to do with pride of ownership?

Practice on Your Own: When you take good care of your things, you are showing gratitude to yourself and to your parents. Remind yourself often to be grateful.

Theme: Teamwork!

Discussion: What would happen if a team didn't work together? Would they be a team? Would they be successful?

Compare & Contrast: Hockey and swimming are team sports. Compare how each is scored. Remember: everyone has to work together in order to get points.

Connection to Self: *Journal writing.* Finish this sentence: "A time when I gave my best effort was _____."

Young-Thinker Activity (K-2): Divide the class into two teams and put each team into its own line. The goal is to pass a spoon with a ping pong ball on it through the line. If the ping pong ball falls, the ball has to go back to the front of the line. The team that is able to pass the ping pong ball through the line without dropping it wins. Afterward, discuss how each can show their gratefulness to their teammates.

In-depth Activity (3-5): Divide the class into two teams and put each team into its own line. The goal is to pass a spoon with a ping pong ball on it through the line. If the ping pong ball falls, the ball has to go back to the front of the line. The team that is able to pass the ping pong ball through the line without dropping it wins. Afterward, discuss how each can show their gratefulness to their teammates.

Practice on Your Own: Remind yourself to be grateful every day.

Theme: Working on partner projects

Decide to start today.
Hug your grandma and grandpa when they help you.

Discussion: Why is it important to be able to work with another person? Do we work with partners only at school? Name other places/events where two people have to work together to achieve a goal.

Compare & Contrast: Imagine you have to build a dog house all by yourself. How would you start? What would you do? Now, imagine that an adult is going to help you. Now how would you start? What would you do? What are the differences between when we work with someone and when we work alone?

Connection to Self: *Journal writing.* Describe a time when you worked with one other person on a school project. How did it go? Were there problems? If so, how did you resolve them?

Young-Thinker Activity (K-2): Sometimes it's hard for kids to work together because they feel like they have nothing in common. Pair students and have each interview the other using the **H5 Who Are You? Skills Page** (pg. 135). Star the answers that are the same.

In-depth Activity (3-5): *Journal writing.* Describe a partner project you worked on in the past. What was the project? Which parts did you do? Which parts did your partner do? What did you learn from that experience? Would you do anything differently next time?

Practice on Your Own: Remind yourself, "Practice, practice, and never give up!"

Theme: How can you help a sibling or friend?

Thank your brother or sister for helping you do your homework.

Discussion: Do you have siblings or friends who ask for help? Do you ever help them? How do you help them? How do you feel after you've helped someone? How do you think they feel?

Compare & Contrast: What are the emotions you feel when you need to ask for help? What are the emotions you feel when you get help? Are there any similarities?

—◦⟋⟍⟍⟋⟍⟍◦⟋⟍⟍◦⟍⟍◦⟍⟍◦⟍⟍◦⟍⟍◦⟋⟍⟍⟋⟍⟍◦⟍⟍◦⟍⟍◦⟍⟍◦—

Connection to Self: *Journal writing.* Finish this sentence: "I've asked for help from _____ because _____." Give details about what happened.

Young-Thinker Activity (K-2): Draw a picture of the best place to do homework in your house. Make sure you have everything you need. Draw a clock in your picture that shows the time you do your homework and then be sure to include where you put your homework when it's finished.

In-depth Activity (3-5): Set up a corner in your room where students can help other students. Maybe determine who could be a mentor and make a list of available students. Instruct the kids that when they see someone approach the corner, if they are next on the list to help that they should help their peer. High-fives should be given to both students.

—◦⟋⟍⟍⟋⟍⟍◦⟋⟍⟍◦⟍⟍◦⟍⟍◦⟍⟍◦⟍⟍◦⟋⟍⟍⟋⟍⟍◦⟍⟍◦⟍⟍◦⟍⟍◦—

Practice on Your Own: Make a list of who you could ask for help. Keep the list handy for when you need help.

H5 Skills Pages

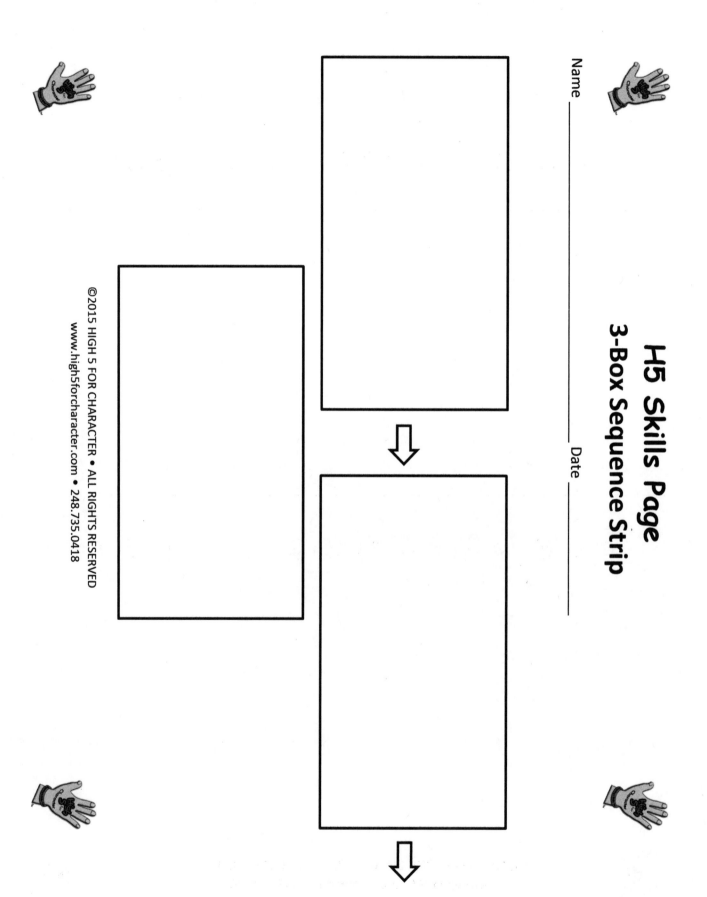

H5 Skills Page
3-Box Sequence Strip

Name _____

Date _____

H5 Skills Page
5 Ways to Lend a Hand

Name _____ Date _____

1. Name a way to help someone while sitting down: _____
   _____
   _____

2. Name a way to help someone without saying a word:_____
   _____
   _____

3. Name a way to help someone while walking: _____
   _____
   _____

4. Name a way to help someone while running: _____
   _____
   _____

5. Name a way to help someone while in the car: _____
   _____
   _____

H5 Skills Page

Becoming a Better Me! Asking for Help

Name _____ Date _____

What I Need Help With...	Who I Can Ask...

H5 Skills Page
Becoming a Better Me! Chart

Name _____

Date _____

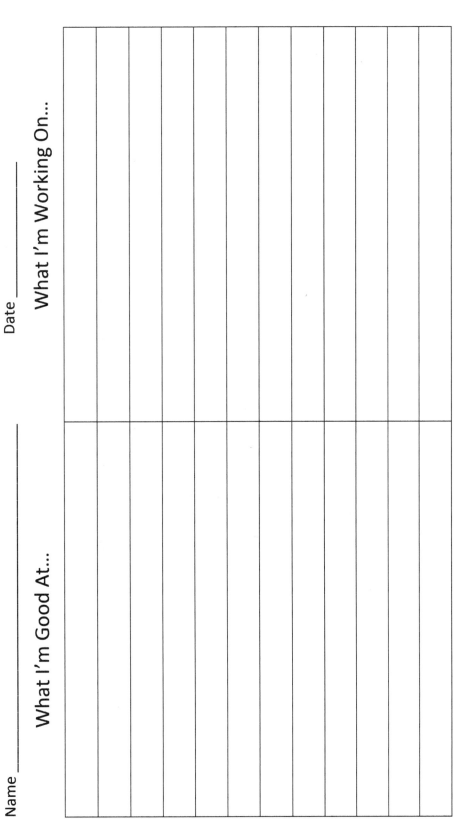

What I'm Good At...	What I'm Working On...

H5 Skills Page
Clean and Tidy!

Name _____ Date _____

```
V T A N T S B U G S
J F K D F L O W E R
V N W I Z C L C A T
N X J N Z R E Q G P
T D B C Y J Z Q E B
L Y G W A T E R A C
A J A M K A O N O U
K Z I D O G B I R D
E S R R I V E R X I
C T R E E S F I S H
```

trees	fish	lake	river	air
water	flower	cat	dog	bird
ants	bugs			

H5 Skills Page
Clean and Tidy! Answer Key

Clean and Tidy!

```
V T A N T S B U G S
J F K D F L O W E R
V N W I Z C L C A T
N X J N Z R E Q G P
T D B C Y J Z Q E B
L Y G W A T E R A C
A J A M K A O N O U
K Z I D O G B I R D
E S R R I V E R X I
C T R E E S F I S H
```

trees	fish	lake	river	air
water	flower	cat	dog	bird
ants	bugs			

H5 Skills Page
C-O-N-F-I-D-E-N-T Acrostic

Name _____ Date _____

C _____

O _____

N _____

F _____

I _____

D _____

E _____

N _____

T _____

H5 Skills Page
C-O-N-F-I-D-E-N-T Acrostic Word List

To help students complete the **H5 C-O-N-F-I-D-E-N-T Acrostic Skills Page**, use this sheet to help identify the correct word for each letter.

CARE	CAT	CAR	CAMP
ONION	OPTIMISTIC	OILY	OREO
NASTY	NICE	NAP	NOBODY
FRIEND	FORK	FAST	FIND
ICE	INK	IMAGINE	IMPORTANT
DOG	DARE	DEEP	DEPENDABLE
EGG	EAGER	EYE	EARTH
NEAT	NEXT	NO	NOODLE
TRUST	TROUBLE	TRUCK	TABLE

H5 Skills Page
Cookie!

Name _____ Date _____

Decorate your cookie! Who would you like to share it with? Write their names on the line below.

I want to share my cookie with _____.

H5 Skills Page
Donate vs. Trash

Name _____ Date _____

Put the following words in the correct column.

banana peel   clean clothes   gently used clothes   unbroken toys

boots   empty potato chip bag   empty juice box   scarf

Donate	Put in trash

Add other words when you're finished with the word list. Where could you donate your items?

_____

H5 Skills Page
Do's & Don'ts Word Search

Name _____ Date _____

```
L K A F L L L U E U C L U L G
L G Q Z R Q Z R H Z Q S S I T
W L R M C Q H E C B B P U S H
W W U B F U D L Y E L L A T Q
H P R U N I B F Z J H E E E F
B C O H T E I V X G H J O N H
Q I E S S T V D G U C I C R B
S S K H L H P R X I O J V B D
M A M A P Z Y P S C Z S U A Y
E Z W R S H Y L W M A U Z R K
U U O E T O H B R N J J G G L
V T U A E S S B G R W H R R A
A I Z G A H Z F Q R X S M H W
I S S O L P S I X R B S M V A
X W Q V W E G I Y K W F T X U
```

yell	run	push	steal	grab
listen	sit	walk	share	quiet

H5 Skills Page
Do's & Don'ts Answer Key

Do's & Don'ts

```
L K A F L L L U E U C L U L G
L G Q Z R Q Z R H Z Q S S I T
W L R M C Q H E C B B P U S H
W W U B F U D L Y E L L A T Q
H P R U N I B F Z J H E E E F
B C O H T E I V X G H J O N H
Q I E S S T V D G U C I C R B
S S K H L H P R X I O J V B D
M A M A P Z Y P S C Z S U A Y
E Z W R S H Y L W M A U Z R K
U U O E T O H B R N J J J G G L
V T U A E S S B G R W H R R A
A I Z G A H Z F Q R X S M H W
I S S O L P S I X R B S M V A
X W Q V W E G I Y K W F T X U
```

yell	run	push	steal	grab
listen	sit	walk	share	quiet

H5 Skills Page
Double Hand

Name

Date

H5 Skills Page
E-M-P-A-T-H-Y Acrostic

Name _____ Date _____

E _____

M_____

P _____

A _____

T _____

H_____

Y _____

H5 Skills Page
E-M-P-A-T-H-Y Acrostic Word List

To help students complete the **H5 E-M-P-A-T-H-Y Acrostic Skills Page**, use this sheet to help identify the correct word for each letter.

EQUAL	ENDLESS	ERASER	EGGROLL
MONKEY	MASK	MINDFUL	MOLAR
PIG	PATIENT	PEN	PINEAPPLE
ACTION	ART	APPLE	ARROW
TRICK	TRIP	TURTLE	TRUE
HAPPY	HAT	HEAVY	HARD
YODEL	YELLOW	YOU	YARN

H5 Skills Page
G-R-A-T-E-F-U-L Acrostic

Name _____ Date _____

G _____

R _____

A _____

T _____

E _____

F _____

U _____

L _____

H5 Skills Page
G-R-A-T-E-F-U-L Acrostic Word List

To help students complete the **H5 G-R-A-T-E-F-U-L Acrostic Skills Page**, use this sheet to help identify the correct word for each letter.

GIVE	GATE	GRUMPY	GRAPE
RED	RIDICULE	RAIN	RESPONSIBLE
APPLE	APPRECIATE	ANKLE	ALLOW
THANKFUL	TANK	TOP	TALK
EDGE	EASEL	EVE	EASY
FAKE	FRIEND	FLIP	FAN
UGLY	UNICORN	UNDER	UNDERSTAND
LEG	LOVE	LARK	LIVER

H5 Skills Page
Gratefulness Challenge

Name _____ Date _____

For five days, keep track of people and times that have made you feel grateful. Record the date and the name of the person or the action that made you feel grateful.

Day 1 Date: _____

Person or action that made me feel grateful: _____

_____

Day 2 Date: _____

Person or action that made me feel grateful: _____

_____

Day 3 Date: _____

Person or action that made me feel grateful: _____

_____

Day 4 Date: _____

Person or action that made me feel grateful: _____

_____

Day 5 Date: _____

Person or action that made me feel grateful: _____

_____

H5 Skills Page
Hand

Name _____ Date _____

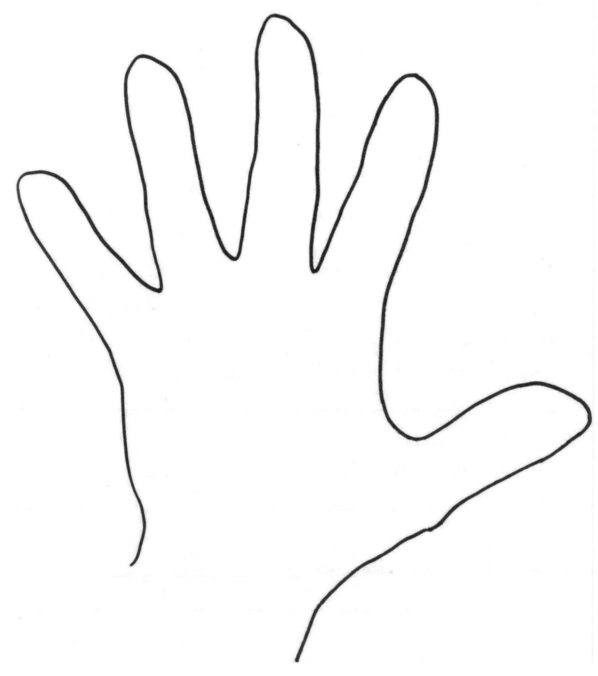

H5 High 5ver!

_____

(Student Name)

showed GREAT character by

_____

(Action)

_____ CUT HERE _____

H5 High 5ver!

_____

(Student Name)

showed GREAT character by

_____

(Action)

H5 Skills Page
H-O-N-E-S-T Acrostic

Name _____ Date _____

H _____

O _____

N _____

E _____

S _____

T _____

H5 Skills Page
H-O-N-E-S-T Acrostic Word List

To help students complete the **H5 H-O-N-E-S-T Acrostic Skills Page**, use this sheet to help identify the correct word for each letter.

HANK	HONORABLE	HAT	HAIRY
OPEN	OIL	ONION	OAR
NAP	NECK	NICE	NOODLE
EQUAL	END	EGGROLL	EASEL
SHIP	SEAGULL	SAW	SINCERE
TRUE	TAN	TRUCK	TABLE

Every Day Is A Character Day Activity Book

H5 Skills Page
How I Feel

Name _____ Date _____

Complete each face with a different emotion (happiness, sadness, fear, surprise, etc.). On the line, write a sentence about when you felt this emotion.

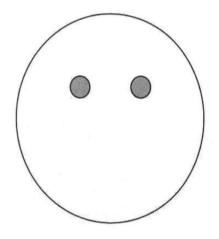
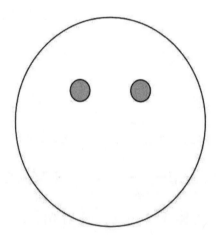

_____   _____

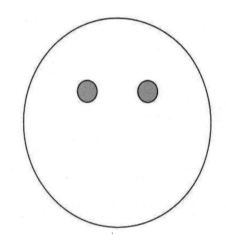
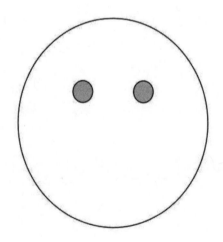

_____   _____

H5 Skills Page
I Am _____ Web Diagram

Name _____ Date _____

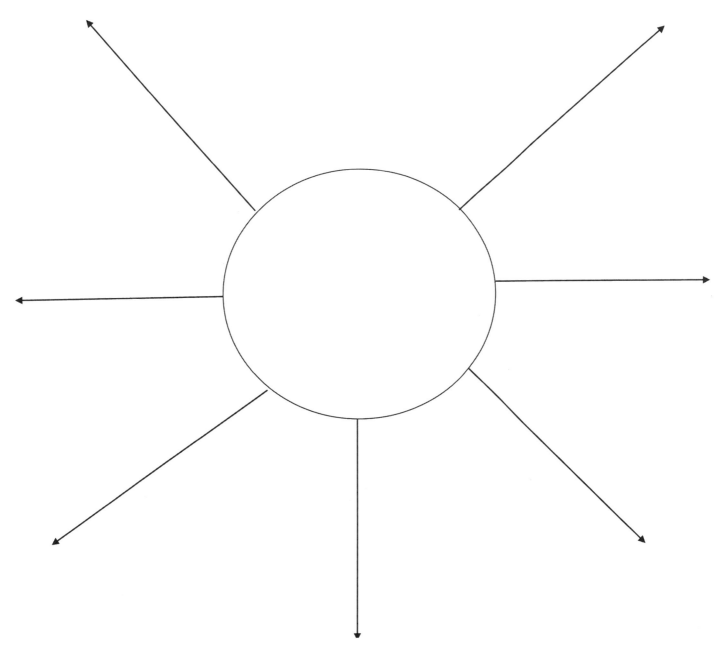

H5 Skills Page
I'm a Helper Word Search

Name _____ Date _____

```
H X I O P Y P A Z K F Q P A G
M Q I O L T S C A R R Y U S Z
O W Y M K K Y R Y F F Z Z V P
H Q L Y V Z X B O O K S D O D
Z T M B A C K P A C K S D L D
M G V J C R U T C H E S Y G F
B R O K E N L E G O N Y Y W S
H V K B O U S L H B M M L P T
E A T Z N U U F R I E N D G T
L A S N W N I L B J Z S I N H
P M Q G C S C P Q Q G V M C U
Z N E H A P E L R M E V Z D Z
C N F B G M N H K G Y R J R Q
V L M P R C A S T G L B H Q H
Q Z T I M X I L O X I B T S Q
```

broken leg   **crutches**   **cast**   **backpack**   **lunch**

books   **help**   **carry**   **friend**   **give**

H5 Skills Page
I'm a Helper Answer Key

I'm A Helper

```
H X I O P Y P A Z K F Q P A G
M Q I O L T S C A R R Y U S Z
O W Y M K K Y R Y F F Z Z V P
H Q L Y V Z X B O O K S D O D
Z T M B A C K P A C K S D L D
M G V J C R U T C H E S Y G F
B R O K E N L E G O N Y Y W S
H V K B O U S L H B M M L P T
E A T Z N U U F R I E N D G T
L A S N W N I L B J Z S I N H
P M Q G C S C P Q Q G V M C U
Z N E H A P E L R M E V Z D Z
C N F B G M N H K G Y R J R Q
V L M P R C A S T G L B H Q H
Q Z T I M X I L O X I B T S Q
```

brokenleg	crutches	cast	backpack	lunch
books	help	carry	friend	give

H5 Skills Page
I Am a Patient Kid

Name _____   Date _____

Draw two pictures showing how you are patient. You can close your eyes and count to ten, think happy thoughts about your pet or friend. You can hum a song you already know or breathe through your nose and watch it grow.

Draw a picture of when you had to wait in a long line to get ice cream and how you were patient.

Draw a picture of when you had to wait for your birthday party to start and how you were patient.

H5 Skills Page
I Am Grateful for...

Name _____ Date _____

Name 10 things in your life that you are grateful for. Update monthly.

1.

2.

3.

4.

5.

6.

7.

8.

9.

10.

H5 Skills Page
I Am Grateful for YOU!

Name _____ Date _____

```
F W E Z A U N T D I O L X T X
H A M S T E R H B Z T W L L Q
L E O K P S U M N H S D A U O
I M B X S I S T E R A P J C C
B G L Z A I L H O F I Q H G B
R T E P B L M T I C T M L Z R
A R K X K U H S N M F J J W O
R J E H L Z N I O Y E C A T T
I W G Z V O R N K U R G U C H
A A X Z M P D S Y J R A K F E
N V F R I E N D I V M S W L R
Q H U N C L E R O Q L T C U K
W O S V T E A C H E R C A M I
I J B M O M Z X C P E D A D Y
T D D O G P W N E I G H B O R
```

Mom	Dad	Sister	Friend	Teacher
Brother	Uncle	Aunt	Dog	Cat
Hamster	Bunny	Neighbor	Principal	Librarian

H5 Skills Page
I Am Grateful for YOU! Answer Key

I Am Grateful for YOU!

```
F W E Z A U N T D I O L X T X
H A M S T E R H B Z T W L L Q
L E O K P S U M N H S D A U O
I M B X S I S T E R A P J C C
B G L Z A I L H O F I Q H G B
R T E P B L M T I C T M L Z R
A R K X K U H S N M F J J W O
R J E H L Z N I O Y E C A T T
I W G Z V O R N K U R G U C H
A A X Z M P D S Y J R A K F E
N V F R I E N D I V M S W L R
Q H U N C L E R O Q L T C U K
W O S V T E A C H E R C A M I
I J B M O M Z X C P E D A D Y
T D D O G P W N E I G H B O R
```

Mom	Dad	Sister	Friend	Teacher
Brother	Uncle	Aunt	Dog	Cat
Hamster	Bunny	Neighbor	Principal	Librarian

H5 Skills Page
I Am Honest Word Search

Name _____ Date _____

```
N J E I K V H K C O W Y G V R
K B J O T S E U Z F F A I R O
C Z O Z R I A Y F Z A V O C B
P D S E U L R Y X T N Y F U E
O H P Y T J T E J R L H C N K
P L G Q H G E C N O Y I S C H
R L T B S D G H N U W T E A Z
A N D D V R D E V B J S P H F
C Q J B Q F Y A H L V P E O Z
T I N H O Z S T U E Y N O N P
I L R G F K R B D J L U L E B
C R X K Q O R C D M K Y K S T
E M T K L Y P W V W D Y M T R
K M R G D Y Z M H F I E S K Y
Z U W O Q I I Q R M R Q R R Z
```

fair	truth	trouble	honest	lie
try	practice	happy	cheat	heart

H5 Skills Page
I Am Honest Answer Key

I Am Honest

```
N J E I K V H K C O W Y G V R
K B J O T S E U Z F F A I R O
C Z O Z R I A Y F Z A V O C B
P D S E U L R Y X T N Y F U E
O H P Y T J T E J R L H C N K
P L G Q H G E C N O Y I S C H
R L T B S D G H N U W T E A Z
A N D D V R D E V B J S P H F
C Q J B Q F Y A H L V P E O Z
T I N H O Z S T U E Y N O N P
I L R G F K R B D J L U L E B
C R X K Q O R C D M K Y K S T
E M T K L P W V W D Y M T R
K M R G D Y Z M H F I E S K Y
Z U W O Q I I Q R M R Q R R Z
```

fair	truth	trouble	honest	lie
try	practice	happy	cheat	heart

H5 Skills Page
I Am Respectful Word Search

Name _____ Date _____

```
Y O U ' R E W E L C O M E K E
G M U L N P W W J T I P K O L
K I I Y L S N Z K S C K N G J
B T M D Y C J E R X B W K D L
J N W S W Z E J D T Q B R F U
Y B V Z H O N E S T L K E B R
G B L A Y Z I Z F C M J C C X
L I S T E N P L E A S E A N N
O T H A N K Y O U C H O R E S
J C N U W Z P H A G X A I G E
W M C A Q L U O S G I B N Q R
K I N D N E S S L I D C G C D
E F H E L P F U L I H B Q C G
A P A T I E N T P M T P J M M
H A P P Y J R K R O F E D U I
```

thank you	kindness	helpful	chores	honest
caring	polite	happy	listen	patient
please	you're welcome			

H5 Skills Page
I Am Respectful Answer Key

I Am Respectful

```
Y O U ' R E W E L C O M E K E
G M U L N P W W J T I P K O L
K I I Y L S N Z K S C K N G J
B T M D Y C J E R X B W K D L
J N W S W Z E J D T Q B R F U
Y B V Z H O N E S T L K E B R
G B L A Y Z I Z F C M J C C X
L I S T E N P L E A S E A N N
O T H A N K Y O U C H O R E S
J C N U W Z P H A G X A I G E
W M C A Q L U O S G I B N Q R
K I N D N E S S L I D C G C D
E F H E L P F U L I H B Q C G
A P A T I E N T P M T P J M M
H A P P Y J R K R O F E D U I
```

thankyou	kindness	helpful	chores	honest
caring	polite	happy	listen	patient
please	you'rewelcome			

H5 Skills Page
I Care! Word Search

Name _____ Date _____

```
D G X D A D X D O G F R T I N
V L A O D K I X J Y H V U C H
J Y J S X T H W I L H Y U A G
L H D V G P A U N T X O A T J
D Q Y V C J S U C B M Z P K H
S W E B Q Q X H M V X N D N D
I A Q R O B K A Q Z V M N V N
Y M A R I C E T P H H O A F Y
L D G E P R E P P U N M R N T
L N D H J V L C B T E F G U C
C A C T X U C W U B J N V E Y
R R Q O W W N C E P J G X E J
H G F R R D U S I S T E R P T
Y G H B N I O X P D E G M A K
P J T E A C H E R F R I E N D
```

mom	dad	sister	brother	teacher
uncle	aunt	grandma	grandpa	friend
dog	cat			

H5 Skills Page
I Care! Answer Key

I Care

```
D G X D A D X D O G F R T I N
V L A O D K I X J Y H V U C H
J Y J S X T H W I L H Y U A G
L H D V G P A U N T X O A T J
D Q Y V C J S U C B M Z P K H
S W E B Q Q X H M V X N D N D
I A Q R O B K A Q Z V M N V N
Y M A R I C E T P H H O A F Y
L D G E P R E P P U N M R N T
L N D H J V L C B T E F G U C
C A C T X U C W U B J N V E Y
R R Q O W W N C E P J G X E J
H G F R R D U S I S T E R P T
Y G H B N I O X P D E G M A K
P J T E A C H E R F R I E N D
```

mom	dad	sister	brother	teacher
uncle	aunt	grandma	grandpa	friend
dog	cat			

H5 Skills Page
I Want To ... Chart

Name _____   Date _____

Inside the top box, write your goal. Use the smaller boxes to show what you will do each day to achieve your goal. Also rate each day by circling CB (confidence booster) or CR (confidence reducer) to track your level of confidence.

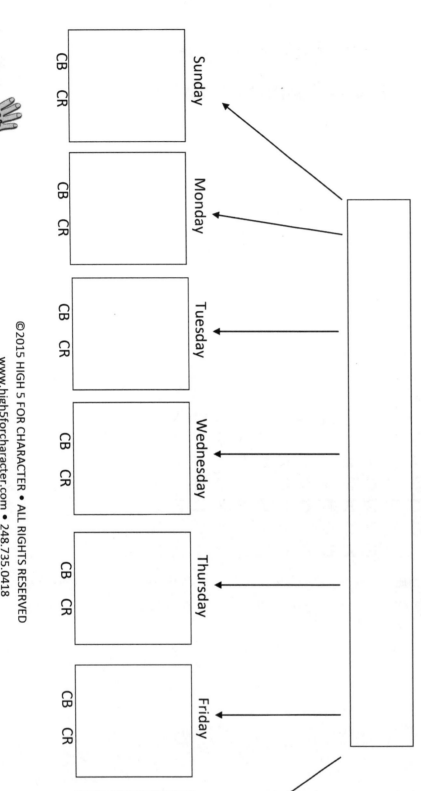

Day	CB	CR
Sunday		
Monday		
Tuesday		
Wednesday		
Thursday		
Friday		
Saturday		

H5 Skills Page
Let's Make Change!

Name _____ Date _____

Imagine you work at a lemonade stand. You sold cups of lemonade for 50 cents and cookies for 25 cents.

How much change would you have to give back in the following situations?

- Someone bought 2 cups of lemonade and 1 cookie and gave you $2.00. *I would give back _____ in change.*

- Someone bought 1 cup of lemonade and gave you $1.00. *I would give back _____ in change.*

- Someone bought 1 cup of lemonade and 2 cookies and gave you $1.00. *I would give back _____ in change.*

- Someone bought 3 cups of lemonade and 3 cookies and gave you $5.00. *I would give back _____ in change.*

H5 Skills Page
Look at My Face! Match

Name _____ Date _____

Match the word with the right face.

Happy

Sad

Surprised

Afraid

Angry

Disappointed

H5 Skills Page
R-E-S-P-E-C-T Acrostic

Name _____ Date _____

R _____

E _____

S _____

P _____

E _____

C _____

T _____

Every Day Is A Character Day Activity Book

H5 Skills Page
R-E-S-P-E-C-T Acrostic Word List

To help students complete the **H5 R-E-S-P-E-C-T Acrostic Skills Page**, use this sheet to help identify the correct word for each letter.

RUDE	RELIABLE	REST	RIGHT
EASY	EAGER	EAT	ELEPHANT
SILLY	SLY	SNEAKY	SMART
PEANUT	PUZZLE	PRACTICE	POPCORN
EMPATHY	ENERGY	EGGROLL	EMPTY
COLD	CALM	CLEVER	CRAZY
TRAIN	TACO	TRACK	TRUST

H5 Skills Page
T-Chart

Name _____ Date _____

H5 Skills Page
True Friend Word Search

Name _____ Date _____

```
X J X L A C H B H I W G R G G
R Z Y A Z G H L X H V Q X A Y
M C T U L G F V O I I X J Q E
R O Z G Q F K D B L J X S O C
T R A H H L U R E J E M I N W
P L A Y I L O Y A L I R Q S P
P W N J W E L N N L F Q J H B
O Y J T R Y M L E X Q D U A M
I U P K I N D I C W G H R R U
B Q G G V R L S V A Y A N E J
V O V U W Y O T T K A P E A O
C F B N G Q C E U I E P G V T
C A R E S P Y N K Z Z Y C V L
B J O Y D F U N E D Y D I Z R
G I G G L E M K F R N B H F A
```

care	listen	share	fun	happy
loyal	kind	laugh	smile	joy
play	giggle			

H5 Skills Page
True Friend Answer Key

True Friend

```
X J X L A C H B H I W G R G G
R Z Y A Z G H L X H V Q X A Y
M C T U L G F V O I I X J Q E
R O Z G Q F K D B L J X S O C
T R A H H L U R E J E M I N W
P L A Y I L O Y A L I R Q S P
P W N J W E L N N L F Q J H B
O Y J T R Y M L E X Q D U A M
I U P K I N D I C W G H R R U
B Q G G V R L S V A Y A N E J
V O V U W Y O T T K A P E A O
C F B N G Q C E U I E P G V T
C A R E S P Y N K Z Z Y C V L
B J O Y D F U N E D Y D I Z R
G I G G L E M K F R N B H F A
```

care	listen	share	fun	happy
loyal	kind	laugh	smile	joy
play	giggle			

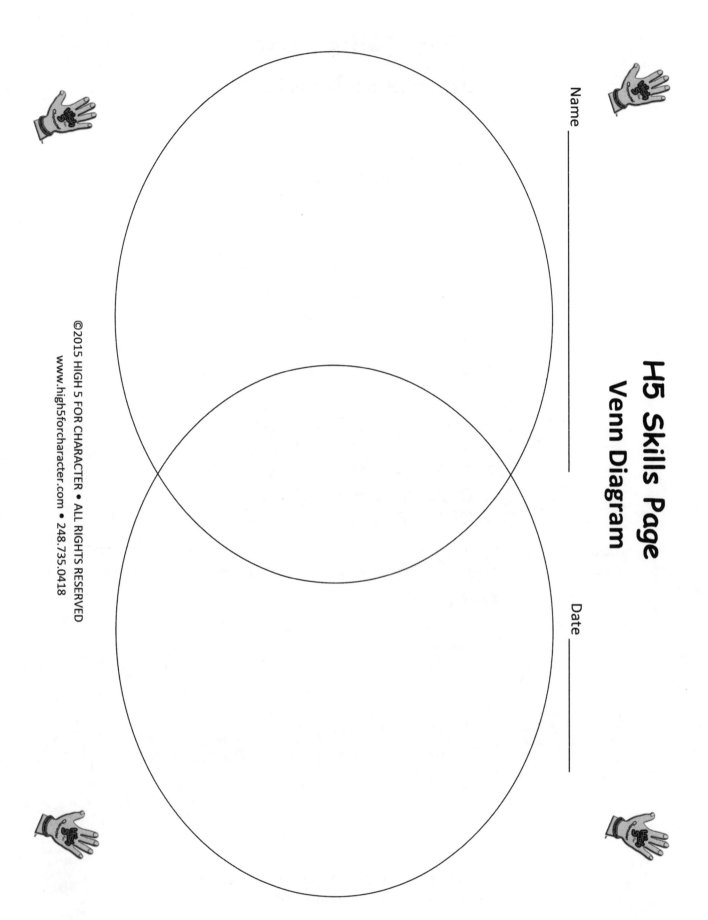

Name _____

Date _____

H5 Skills Page
Venn Diagram

H5 Skills Page
Who Are You?

1. What is your name? _____

2. How old are you? _____

3. Where do you live? _____

4. How tall are you? _____

5. What color are your eyes? _____

6. What color is your hair? _____

7. What do you like to eat the best? _____

8. Do you like ice cream? _____

    a. What kind? _____

9. Do you like pizza? _____

10. Do you like sports? _____

    a. Which ones? _____

11. What subject are you good at in school? _____

12. Would you like to play with me at recess? _____

H5 Skills Page
Who Has Excellent Character? ME!!
Word Search

Name _____ Date _____

```
A V R X H E L P F U L S Y X V K G X N E
C C O N S I D E R A T E W J J R Y S B L
S V E Y S S I T D D H J A Z P Q M L U B
U Q F K B M X I R D R E F N N Y J K E V
T K B O W F V L Y T G Y R L B L J U T G
J L Z R P Z N O G T E X F F N D M J R I
S T E R F N C P B R U X G I V I N G U T
E R U L G E M Z H T C C G Y I G X Z S S
V U I L L T H A R D W O R K I N G G T E
Q T V U A S R I L V Q Y N B H S A N W N
R H C F I I T L X L L H Z F Z G A I O O
E F I E E L Y L P D C V P E I Z Y R R H
S U T T B J Z A N K A S P S J D D A T X
P L E A Y G F E J V V U E D N B E C H L
E T H R A P I F E E L I N G S Z O N Y H
C H T G X R Q M F S C W S I J D G V T A
T H A J F F O F K T F A I S M G K Y M P
F T P A F H K M R E S P O N S I B L E P
U N M J T H Q T H O U G H T F U L I W Y
L C E C H J G K I N D D U Y D U R Q P J
```

confident	respectful	empathetic	honest
grateful	caring	friendly	kind
helpful	thoughtful	giving	hardworking
trustworthy	polite	happy	responsible
feelings	listen	truthful	considerate

H5 Skills Page
Who Has Excellent Character? ME!!
Answer Key

Who Has Excellent Character? ME!!

```
A V R X H E L P F U L S Y X V K G X N E
C C O N S I D E R A T E W J J R Y S B L
S V E Y S S I T D D H J A Z P Q M L U B
U Q F K B M X I R D R E F N N Y J K E V
T K B O W F V L Y T G Y R L B L J U T G
J L Z R P Z N O G T E X F F N D M J R I
S T E R F N C P B R U X G I V I N G U T
E R U L G E M Z H T C C G Y I G X Z S S
V U I L L H A R D W O R K I N G G T E
Q T V U A S R I L V Q Y N B H S A N W N
R H C F I I T L X L L H Z F Z G A I O O
E F I E L Y L P D C V P E I Z Y R R H
S U T T B J Z A N K A S P S J D D A T X
P L E A Y G F E J V V U E D N B E C H L
E T H R A P I F E E L I N G S Z O N Y H
C H T G X R Q M F S C W S I J D G V T A
T H A J F F O K T F A I S M G K Y M P
F T P A F H K M R E S P O N S I B L E P
U N M J T H Q T H O U G H T F U L I W Y
L C E C H J G K I N D D U Y D U R Q P J
```

Confident	Caring	Giving	Responsible	Respectful
Friendly	Hardworking	Feelings	Empathetic	Kind
Trustworthy	Listen	Honest	Helpful	Polite
Truthful	Grateful	Thoughtful	Happy	Considerate

Every Day Is A Character Day Activity Book

H5 Skills Page
WWYD (What Would You Do?)

Name _____ Date _____

Let's think like a confident kid! What is the correct choice for the situations on the left side? Read each situation and draw a line to match the left to the right.

What would you do if you received the lowest test score in the class?	Try to stay focused.
What would you do if your teacher was trying to get the class to be quiet?	Don't listen to those words and tell him/her that you aren't dumb.
What would you do if someone called you dumb?	Lend your classmate a pencil.
What would you do if you raised your hand and didn't have any answer?	Make a plan to study more.
What would you do if someone didn't have a pencil?	Ask for help.
What would you do if someone didn't understand a math problem?	Offer to help.
What would you do if you were having trouble understanding the lesson?	Tell that person that pushing is not how we act in our classroom.
What would you do if someone pushed you out of line?	Set a good example by showing quiet behavior to others.

The Every Day Is A Character Day Activity Book utilizes the following standards:
Common Core Standards

Grades K and 1

Reading Standards for Informational Text—Crafts and Structure	• RI K.5, 1.5 • RI K.6, 1.6 • RI K.3, 1.3 • RI K.7, 1.7 • RI K.1, K.2, 1.1, 1.2 • RI K.3, 1.3
Reading Standards: Foundational Skills—Phonics and Word Recognition	• RF K.3, 1.3
Writing Standards—Text Types and Purposes	• W 1.1 • W1.3
Speaking and Listening Standards—Comprehension and Collaboration	• SL 1.1.a

Grades 2-3

Standard RI: Reading Standards for Informational Text—Key Ideas and Details	• RI 2.1, 2.2 • RI 3.1, 3.2
Standard RI: Reading Standards for Informational Text—Craft and Structure	• RI 2.6 • RI 3.4, 3.6
Standard RI: Reading Standards for Informational Text—Integration of Knowledge and Ideas	• RI 2.7 • RI 2.8 • RI 3.7, 3.8
Standard RF: Reading Standards: Foundational Skills—Phonics and Word Recognition	• RF 2.3 • RF 3.3
Standard RF: Reading Standards: Foundational Skills—Fluency	• RF 2.4
Standard W: Writing Standards—Text Types and Purposes	• W 2.1, 2.3 • W 3.1, 3.3
Standard SL: Speaking and Listening Standards—Comprehension and Collaboration	• SL 2.1, 2.2, 2.3 • SL 3.1, 3.2, 3.3
Standard SL: Speaking and Listening Standards—Presentation of Knowledge and Ideas	• SL 2.4 • SL 3.4
Standard RF: Reading Standards: Foundational Skills—Fluency	• RF 3.4

Grades 4-5

Standard RI: Reading Standards for Informational Text—Key Ideas and Details	• RI 4.1, 4.2 • RI 5.1, 5.2
Standard RI: Reading Standards for Informational Text—Craft and Structure	• RI 4.4, 4.6 • RI 5.4, 5.5, 5.6
Standard RI: Reading Standards for Informational Text—Integration of Knowledge and Ideas	• RI 4.7, 4.8, 4.9 • RI 5.7, 5.8, 5.9
Standard RF: Reading Standards: Foundational Skills—Phonics and Word Recognition	• RF 4.3 • RF 5.3
Standard RF: Reading Standards: Foundational Skills—Fluency	• RF 4.4 • RF 5.4
Standard W: Writing Standards—Text Types and Purposes	• W 4.1, 4.3 • W 5.1, 5.3
Standard W: Writing Standards—Research to Build and Present Knowledge	• W 4.8 • W 5.8
Standard SL: Speaking and Listening Standards—Comprehension and Collaboration	• SL 4.1, 4.2, 4.3 • SL 5.1, 5.2, 5.3
Standard SL: Speaking and Listening Standards—Presentation of Knowledge and Ideas	• SL 4.4 • SL 5.4, 5.5

Illinois State Board of Education—Social Emotional Learning Standards
Grades K and 1

Goal 1 Develop self-awareness and self-management skills to achieve school and life success. 1A Identify and manage one's emotions and behavior.	• 1, 2, 6
1B Recognize personal qualities and external supports.	• 1, 2, 3
Goal 2 Use social-awareness and interpersonal skills to establish and maintain positive relationships. 2A Recognize the feelings and perspectives of others.	• 5
2D Demonstrate an ability to prevent, manage and resolve interpersonal conflicts in constructive ways.	• 1

Illinois State Board of Education—Social Emotional Learning Standards
Grades 2-3

Goal 1 Develop self-awareness and self-management skills to achieve school and life success. 1A Identify and manage one's emotions and behavior.	• 1, 2, 6
1B Recognize personal qualities and external supports.	• 1, 3
1C Demonstrate skills related to achieving personal and academic goals.	• 3, 5
Goal 2 Use social-awareness and interpersonal skills to establish and maintain positive relationships. 2A Recognize the feelings and perspectives of others.	• 3, 5
2B: Recognize individual and group similarities and differences.	• 1
2D Demonstrate an ability to prevent, manage, and resolve interpersonal conflicts in constructive ways.	• 1
Goal 3 Demonstrate decision-making skills and responsible behavior in personal, school, and community contexts. 3A Consider ethical, safety, and societal factors in making decisions.	• 1

Illinois State Board of Education—Social Emotional Learning Standards
Grades 4-5

Goal 1 Develop self-awareness and self-management skills to achieve school and life success. 1A Identify and manage one's emotions and behavior.	• 2, 6, 7
1B Recognize personal qualities and external supports.	• 1,3
1C Demonstrate skills related to achieving personal and academic goals.	• 1, 3
Goal 2 Use social-awareness and interpersonal skills to establish and maintain positive relationships. 2A Recognize the feelings and perspectives of others.	• 1, 5
2B Recognize individual and group similarities and differences.	• 4
2C Use communication and social skills to interact effectively with others.	• 6
2D Demonstrate an ability to prevent, manage, and resolve interpersonal conflicts in constructive ways.	• 6
Goal 3 Demonstrate decision-making skills and responsible behavior in personal, school, and community. 3A Consider ethical, safety, and societal factors in making decisions.	• 3
3B Apply decision-making skills to deal responsibly with daily academic and social situations.	• 3
3C Contribute to the well-being of one's school and community.	• 1

See http://www.isbe.net/ils/social_emotional/standards.htm for full listing of descriptors.

About the Authors

Photo by Eric Yankee

Kris Yankee is the co-founder of High 5 for Character, as well as an editor, writer, and mom. The values presented by High 5 for Character and this new series are those that she and her husband hope to instill in their two children. She is an award-winning author of several titles.

Visit krisyankee.com or find Kris on Facebook and Twitter.

For ten years, Marian Nelson has been the publisher for Nelson Publishing & Marketing with over 165 titles in print. As a veteran educator, Marian keeps her focus on the children of the world, actively pursuing concepts that build healthy character. It is her hope that people will continue to learn, grow, and be inspired by all of the books that we publish.

Visit nelsonpublishingandmarketing.com to see the wide variety of subject matter.

Photo by Eric Yankee

Visit us at high5forcharacter.com.
Like us at facebook.com/High5ForCharacter   Follow us on Twitter @Hi5ForCharacter